Collins

COBUILD
Key Words for
Electrical
Engineering

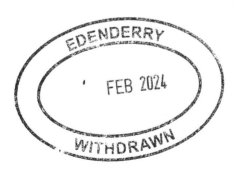

HarperCollins Publishers
Westerhill Road
Bishopbriggs
Glasgow
G64 2QT

First Edition 2013

© HarperCollins Publishers 2013

ISBN 978-0-00-748979-4

Collins® and COBUILD® are
registered trademarks of
HarperCollins Publishers Limited

www.collinselt.com
www.collinsdictionary.com/cobuild

A catalogue record for this book is
available from the British Library

Audio recorded by Networks SRL,
Milan, Italy

Acknowle⸍   ⸌r that the
We would   makes it
and publi   es or bugs.
permissic   ons please
to be used   vided on
We would
Newspape
valuable c

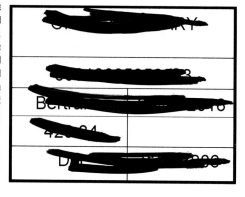

Contents

Contributors

Specialist consultant
Professor Alexander Close (Rtd), Institute of Electrical, Electronic and
Computer Engineering, School of Engineering and Physical Sciences,
Heriot-Watt University

Project manager
Patrick White

Editors
Katherine Carroll
Gavin Gray
Kate Mohideen
Justin Nash
Ruth O'Donovan
Enid Pearsons
Elizabeth Walter
Kate Woodford

Computing support
Mark Taylor

For the publisher
Gerry Breslin
Lucy Cooper
Kerry Ferguson
Elaine Higgleton
Rosie Pearce
Lisa Sutherland

Introduction

Collins COBUILD Key Words for Electrical Engineering is a brand-new vocabulary book for students who want to master the English of Electrical Engineering in order to study or work in the field. This title contains the 500 most important English words and phrases relating to Electrical Engineering, as well as a range of additional features which have been specially designed to help you to *really* understand and use the language of this specific area.

The main body of the book contains alphabetically organized dictionary-style entries for the key words and phrases of Electrical Engineering. These vocabulary items have been specially chosen to fully prepare you for the type of language that you will need in this field. Many are specialized terms that are very specific to this profession and area of study. Others are more common or general words and phrases that are often used in the context of Electrical Engineering.

Each word and phrase is explained clearly and precisely, in English that is easy to understand. In addition, each entry is illustrated with examples taken from the Collins Corpus. Of course, you will also find grammatical information about the way that the words and phrases behave.

In amongst the alphabetically organized entries, you will find valuable word-building features that will help you gain a better understanding of this area of English. For example, some features provide extra help with tricky pronunciations, while others pull together groups of related words that can usefully be learned as a set.

At the start of this book you will see lists of words and phrases, helpfully organized by topic area. You can use these lists to revise sets of vocabulary and to prepare for writing tasks. You can also download the audio for this book from www.collinselt.com/audio. This contains a recording of each headword in the book, followed by an example sentence. This will help you to learn and remember pronunciations of words and phrases. Furthermore, the exercise section at the end of this book gives you an opportunity to memorize important words and phrases, to assess what you have learned, and to work out which areas still need attention.

So whether you are studying Electrical Engineering, or you are already working in the field and intend to improve your career prospects, we are confident that *Collins COBUILD Key Words for Electrical Engineering* will equip you for success in the future.

Guide to Dictionary Entries

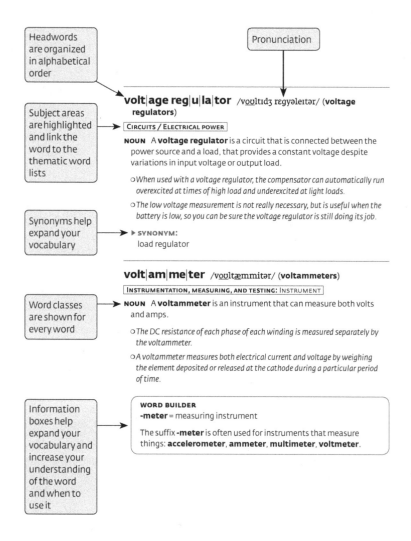

Headwords are organized in alphabetical order

Pronunciation

Subject areas are highlighted and link the word to the thematic word lists

Synonyms help expand your vocabulary

Word classes are shown for every word

Information boxes help expand your vocabulary and increase your understanding of the word and when to use it

volt|age reg|u|la|tor /vˈoʊltɪdʒ rˈɛɡyəleɪtər/ (**voltage regulators**)

CIRCUITS / ELECTRICAL POWER

NOUN A **voltage regulator** is a circuit that is connected between the power source and a load, that provides a constant voltage despite variations in input voltage or output load.

○ *When used with a voltage regulator, the compensator can automatically run overexcited at times of high load and underexcited at light loads.*

○ *The low voltage measurement is not really necessary, but is useful when the battery is low, so you can be sure the voltage regulator is still doing its job.*

▸ **SYNONYM:**
 load regulator

volt|am|me|ter /vˈoʊltæmmitər/ (**voltammeters**)

INSTRUMENTATION, MEASURING, AND TESTING: INSTRUMENT

NOUN A **voltammeter** is an instrument that can measure both volts and amps.

○ *The DC resistance of each phase of each winding is measured separately by the voltammeter.*

○ *A voltammeter measures both electrical current and voltage by weighing the element deposited or released at the cathode during a particular period of time.*

WORD BUILDER
-meter = measuring instrument

The suffix **-meter** is often used for instruments that measure things: **accelerometer**, **ammeter**, **multimeter**, **voltmeter**.

Guide to Dictionary Entries

back E|M|F /bæk i ɛm ɛf/ (short for **back electromotive force**)

Variants of the headword, such as abbreviated, full forms and British forms, are also shown

ELECTRICAL POWER: MOTOR OR GENERATOR

NOUN **Back EMF** is the system in the coil of an electric motor that opposes the current flowing through the coil, when the armature rotates.

Definitions explain what the word means in simple language

○ When the speed varies, the winding characteristics may fluctuate, resulting in variation of back EMF.

○ At high speeds the traction motor armatures are rotating rapidly and have a high back EMF.

Examples show how the word is used in context

trans|mit /trænzmɪt/ (**transmits, transmitted, transmitting**)

All the different forms of the word are listed

COMMUNICATION

VERB If a device **transmits** power or a signal, it sends information, normally in the form of electrical signals. The symbol for transmit is Tx.

○ The high side is connected in a star configuration so that the power generated by the power plant can be transmitted over long distances economically.

○ The modem modulates a signal being transmitted and demodulates a signal being received.

▶ **COLLOCATIONS:**
transmit power
transmit a signal

Collocations help you put the word into practice

Guide to Pronunciation Symbols

Vowel Sounds

ɑ	calm, ah
ɑr	heart, far
æ	act, mass
aɪ	dive, cry
aɪər	fire, tire
aʊ	out, down
aʊər	flour, sour
ɛ	met, lend, pen
eɪ	say, weight
ɛər	fair, care
ɪ	fit, win
i	feed, me
ɪər	near, beard
ɒ	lot, spot
oʊ	note, coat
ɔ	claw, bought
ɔr	more, cord
ɔɪ	boy, joint
ʊ	could, stood
u	you, use
ʊər	lure, endure
ɜr	turn, third
ʌ	fund, must
ə	*the first vowel in* **a**bout
ər	*the first vowel in* **fo**rgotten
i	*the second vowel in* ver**y**
u	*the second vowel in* act**u**al

Consonant Sounds

b	bed, rub
d	done, red
f	fit, if
g	good, dog
h	hat, horse
y	yellow, you
k	king, pick
l	lip, bill
ᵊl	handle, panel
m	mat, ram
n	not, tin
ᵊn	hidden, written
p	pay, lip
r	run, read
s	soon, bus
t	talk, bet
v	van, love
w	win, wool
w	why, wheat
z	zoo, buzz
ʃ	ship, wish
ʒ	measure, leisure
ŋ	sing, working
tʃ	cheap, witch
θ	thin, myth
ð	then, other
dʒ	joy, bridge

Word lists

CIRCUITS

admittance
ampere
ampere-turn
amplitude
angular velocity
anode
attenuation
bidirectional
bit
block diagram
Boolean algebra
breakdown
byte
capacitance
capacitor
cathode
clock
coaxial cable
complex number
conductance
conductivity
conductor
conductor loss
copper loss
coulomb
current
current rating
damping
data
decade
decibel
digital meter
direct current
discharge
dummy load
electric charge
electric current
electric field
electric flux
electric flux density
electric strength
electrolysis
electrolyte
electromagnetic
electromagnetic
  compatibility
electromagnetic field
electron
electron volt
electrostatic

energy
equipotential
farad
fault current
fault-tolerant
field
Fourier analysis
Fourier series
frequency
frequency spectrum
grounding
henry
hysteresis
imaginary operator
impedance
impulse
inductance
inductor
insulation
insulator
isolation
isolation transformer
isolator
line
live
live wire
load
losses
magnetic flux
megahertz
megavolt
megawatt
microamp
milliamp
nanovolt
noise
normally-closed
normally-open
ohm
Ohm's law
open circuit
peak
peak-to-peak value
period
periodic function
permeability
permittivity
phase difference
polyphase
portable equipment
power

power supply
primary winding
reactance
reactive power
rectification
rectifier
rectify
relay
reluctance
resistance
resistive
rheostat
ripple
RMS
rpm
series
shielding
short circuit
short circuit current
signal
sine wave
single-phase
sinusoid
solenoid
switch
toroid
transformer
transient
transient response
transmission line
voltage regulator
volt-ampere
waveform
winding
wire

COMMUNICATION

antenna
bandwidth
bidirectional
broadband
carrier wave
coaxial cable
decade
dual-band
DVB
earphone
electromagnetic
Fourier analysis
Fourier series
frequency spectrum

HDTV
high frequency
imaginary operator
loading coil
megahertz
microamp
microphone
microwave
milliamp
nanovolt
noise
radio
receiver
RF
RFI
signal
sine wave
skin effect
television
transceiver
transient
transient response
transmit
transmitter
twisted pair
very high frequency
waveform

Analog
amplitude modulation
audio frequency
convolution
demodulation
Fourier transform
frequency modulation
harmonic distortion
Laplace transform
modem
modulate
modulation

Digital
asymmetric digital
  subscriber line
Bluetooth
Wi-Fi

COMPUTING AND
CONTROL
amplification
amplifier

analog
analog to digital
  converter
attenuation
attenuator
automatic gain control
bandpass filter
bandstop filter
bit
block diagram
Boolean algebra
byte
capacitance
capacitor
Category 5
clock
complex number
conductor
controller
current
damping
data
decibel
digital
digital meter
direct current
dummy load
electric charge
electric current
electric field
electric strength
electrolyte
electromagnetic
  compatibility
electron
electron volt
electrostatic
energy
equipotential
farad
feedback
frequency
frequency response
gain
henry
high-pass filter
impedance
impulse
inductance
inductor
input/output

line
load
losses
negative feedback
normally-closed
normally-open
ohm
Ohm's law
op amp
open circuit
period
periodic function
permittivity
phase difference
polyphase
port
portable equipment
positive feedback
power
power supply
primary winding
reactance
rectification
rectifier
rectify
relay
reluctance
remote control
repeater
resistance
resistive
response time
RMS
servo
servomechanism
shielding
short circuit
signal
sine wave
solenoid
steady-state
  response
switch
synchro
toroid
transducer
transfer
transfer function
transformer
transient
transient response

waveform
wire

Digital
address
AND gate
arithmetic logic unit
binary coded decimal
binary notation
bit error rate
bus
CPU
data acquisition
  system
data processing
  equipment
digital to analog
  converter
disk
EPROM
flip flop
Karnaugh map
LSB
parity bit

ELECTRICAL POWER
actuator
air discharge
ampere
ampere-hour
ampere-turn
amplitude
angular velocity
apparent power
block diagram
brake horsepower
breakdown
capacitance
capacitor
circuit breaker
coil
conductance
conductivity
conductor
conductor loss
contactor
copper loss
corona discharge
coulomb
current
current rating

damping
delta connection
digital meter
direct current
discharge
double insulation
dummy load
eddy currents
electric charge
electric current
electric field
electric flux
electric flux density
electric strength
electrolysis
electrolyte
electromagnet
electromagnetic
  compatibility
electromagnetic field
electron
electron volt
electrostatic
energy
equipotential
ESD
farad
fault current
fault-tolerant
field
flux linkage
frequency
full wave rectifier
grounded neutral
grounding
ground leakage
henry
hysteresis
impedance
impulse
inductance
induction coil
induction heating
inductor
installation
insulation
insulator
isolation
isolation transformer
isolator
leakage current

lightning rod
line
live
live wire
load
losses
low-tension
magnetic flux
magnetomotive force
megavolt
megawatt
network
neutral
normally-closed
normally-open
ohm
Ohm's law
open circuit
overcurrent detection
peak
peak-to-peak value
period
periodic function
permeability
permittivity
per unit
phase difference
plant
polyphase
portable equipment
power
power plant
power supply
primary winding
rating
reactance
reactive power
rectification
rectifier
rectify
relay
reluctance
resistance
resistive
rheostat
ripple
RMS
rpm
series
shielding
short circuit

short circuit current
single-phase
sinusoid
solenoid
star connection
switch
switch
three-phase
toroid
transformer
transmission line
voltage regulator
volt-ampere
winding
wire

Distribution
armored cable
balanced three-phase
base load
blackout
brownout
busbar
capacity
demand
distribution line
distribution system
flashover
grid
high-tension
high voltage
outage
power factor
power factor
  correction
power grid
power line
pylon
substation
switchgear
switching station
transmission

Generation
breeder reactor
CHP
core loss
distributed generation
electric system
generate
generation

generator
geothermal power
hydroelectric
nuclear power
power station
renewable energy
solar power
supply
tidal power
turbine
turbo-electric
turbogenerator
wave farm
wave power
wind farm
wind power

Motor or generator
alternator
armature
asynchronous
back EMF
carbon brush
commutator
dynamo
electric motor
engine
excite
field winding
full load current
induction motor
lag
lead
motor
motor generator set
pole piece
rotor
series motor
series-wound
shunt
shunt motor
shunt-wound
slip
slip ring
squirrel cage
starter
stator
synchronous converter
synchronous machine
synchronous speed

Power consumption
appliance
consumer unit
ground leakage circuit
  breaker
kilowatt-hour
lagging load
load
load factor
loss
outlet
overload
peak load
power point
regulation
residual current device
ring circuit
ring main
surge
switchboard

Transformers
autotransformer
lamination
secondary winding
step-down
step-up

ELECTRONICS COMPONENTS
bridge rectifier
bypass capacitor
capacitive crosstalk
choke
coupling capacitor
DC potentiometer
diode
electrolytic capacitor
LED
microswitch
photocell
potentiometer
solar cell
transistor

Digital
chip
NOR gate
OR gate

GENERAL
alternating current
ambient temperature
American wire gauge
autotimer
battery
battery backup
breadboard
cable
cable trunking
CAD
calorie
cathode ray tube
Celsius
charge
cm
compact fluorescent
  lamp
conduit
connector
corrosion
device
discharge tube
duct
electricity
electric light
electric polarization
electric shock
electromagnetic
  interference
electromagnetic
  spectrum
electromechanical
electromotive force
equipment
exponent
ferromagnetism
filament
flex
fuse
gigahertz
gram
hertz
jack
joule
junction box
kilogram
lithium battery
megabits

mks system
newton
pascal
phase
plug
potential difference
push button
radian
schematic
second
siemens
socket
susceptance
temperature
uninterruptible power
  supply
variable
volt
watt
weber
wire
wiring

INSTRUMENTATION, MEASURING, AND TESTING
Bode plot
difference amplifier
display
electron gun
liquid-crystal display

Devices
accelerometer
current transformer
GPS
thermocouple
thermostat

Instrument
ammeter
cathode ray
  oscilloscope
DMM
meter
multimeter
oscilloscope
voltammeter
voltmeter

SEMICONDUCTOR AND ELECTRONIC CIRCUITRY
active element
active filter
circuit
coupling coefficient
current source
detector
dielectric
dielectric constant
dielectric heating
dielectric loss
dielectric strength
dry
electrical circuit
fault
FET
ground
ground return
half wave rectifier
heat sink
integrated circuit
large-scale integration
node
printed circuit board
ROM
semiconductor
shutdown
solar panel
solid-state
square wave
system on a chip
VSWR
ZIF

Analog
nodal analysis
parallel resonance
phasor
Q factor
resonance
resonant circuit
series resonance

Digital
charge-coupled device
microprocessor

A–Z

Aa

---

ac|cel|er|om|e|ter /æksɛlərɒmɪtər/ (accelerometers)

INSTRUMENTATION, MEASURING, AND TESTING: DEVICES

NOUN An **accelerometer** is a device for measuring acceleration.

- ○ *When a low-level accelerometer experiences a large, high-frequency, input acceleration beyond its dynamic operating range, the control circuit's prefilter amplification can saturate.*

- ○ *Direct measurement of acceleration is made using an accelerometer, which makes use of the relationship between force, mass, and acceleration.*

---

ac|tive el|e|ment /æktɪv ɛlɪmənt/ (active elements)

SEMICONDUCTOR AND ELECTRONIC CIRCUITRY

NOUN An **active element** is an element capable of generating electrical energy.

- ○ *The essential role of this active element is to magnify an input signal to yield a significantly larger output signal.*

- ○ *An active element is connected to the antenna terminals leading to the receiver or transmitter, as opposed to a parasitic element that modifies the antenna pattern without being connected directly.*

---

ac|tive fil|ter /æktɪv fɪltər/ (active filters)

SEMICONDUCTOR AND ELECTRONIC CIRCUITRY

NOUN An **active filter** is any filter using an op amp.

- ○ *This is a universal active filter which can be configured for a wide range of low-pass, high-pass, and bandpass filters.*

- ○ *An active filter is a filter that has an energy gain greater than one, so that it outputs more energy than it absorbs.*

A

ac|tu|a|tor /ˈæktʃueɪtər/ (**actuators**)

ELECTRICAL POWER

NOUN An **actuator** is the mechanical part of a switch that uses mechanical force to work the switch contacts.

○ The motorized control valve has an electrical actuator directly mounted on the control valve for controlling the flow of material.

○ Smoke dampers are automated with the use of a mechanical motor often referred to as an actuator.

ad|dress /əˈdrɛs/ (**addresses**)

COMPUTING AND CONTROL: DIGITAL

NOUN In any digital memory, the **address** tells you exactly where each piece of digital information is located.

○ The information required can be found at a specific address location in the memory.

○ It is possible to relocate the information to another address within memory.

ad|mit|tance /ædˈmɪtᵊns/

CIRCUITS

NOUN **Admittance** is a measure of how easy it is for a particular voltage to force a current through an electrical component.

○ The lower the admittance of the component, the more difficult it will be to pass current through it.

○ If a circuit has very high admittance it acts like a short circuit.

air dis|charge /ˈɛər dɪstʃɑrdʒ/

ELECTRICAL POWER

NOUN **Air discharge** is a method for testing ESD-protection structures in which the ESD generator is discharged through an air gap between the generator and the device under test.

○ Since air discharge is affected by atmospheric conditions, there are limits specified for temperature, humidity, and atmospheric pressure.

○ If a serious air discharge occurs there may be a smell of ozone in the near vicinity.

al|ter|nat|ing cur|rent (ABBR **AC**) /ɔltərneɪtɪŋ kɜrənt/

NOUN An **alternating current** is a continuous electric current that periodically reverses direction, usually using a sine wave.

○ Alternating current is necessary for the use of transformers.

○ The most commonly used form of alternating current alternates in a sine wave pattern.

al|ter|na|tor /ɔltərneɪtər/ (**alternators**)

ELECTRICAL POWER: MOTOR OR GENERATOR

NOUN An **alternator** is an electrical machine that generates an alternating current.

○ AC power may be produced by using a motor generator set where you use the DC power to run a DC motor which then runs an AC alternator producing true sinusoid wave forms.

○ A low alternator voltage cannot produce maximum motor current that in turn produces the high tractive effort required for acceleration.

am|bi|ent tem|per|a|ture /æmbiənt tɛmprətʃər/

NOUN **Ambient temperature** is the temperature of the air surrounding a component.

○ If the ambient temperature is high or low, some line current may be consumed to control the temperature.

○ This DC current level is based on a maximum temperature rise of the inductor at the maximum rated ambient temperature.

A|mer|i|can wire gauge (ABBR **AWG**) /əmɛrɪkən waɪər geɪdʒ/

NOUN **American wire gauge** is a measure of wire thickness.

○ American wire gauge is a standardized sizing system for electrically conducting wire.

○ In the United States, smaller conductors are measured by American wire gauge, which is a specification for non-ferrous wire diameter, such as copper, aluminum, gold, and silver.

A

am|me|ter /æmmitər/ (ammeters)

| INSTRUMENTATION, MEASURING, AND TESTING: INSTRUMENT |

NOUN An **ammeter** is an instrument for measuring electric current in amps.

○ One type of ammeter measures current using a coil clipped round the current-carrying wire.

○ An ammeter only measures current so by itself cannot give the power measurement.

am|pere (ABBR A) /æmpɪər/ (amperes)

| CIRCUITS / ELECTRICAL POWER |

NOUN An **ampere** is a measure of electrical current.

○ An ampere is the unit of measurement of electrical current produced in a circuit by 1 volt acting through a resistance of 1 ohm.

○ A current of more than 100 amperes is required to turn the car engine for starting.

WORD ORIGINS

This word is named for the French physicist **André-Marie Ampère** (1775–1836) who worked out the relationship between magnetism and electricity.

---

am|pere-hour (ABBR A-h) /æmpɪər aʊər/ (ampere-hours)

| ELECTRICAL POWER |

NOUN An **ampere-hour** is a measure of charge or current flow over time.

○ For the operation of a pacemaker, only a small amount of power is needed, and thus, one can make do with limited battery ampere-hour capacities.

○ Five ampere-hours means a current flow of one ampere for five hours or a current flow of $2\frac{1}{2}$ ampere for 2 hours.

am|pere-turn (ABBR AT) /æmpɪər tɜrn/ (ampere-turns)

| CIRCUITS / ELECTRICAL POWER |

NOUN An **ampere-turn** is the product of the number of turns in a coil and the current in amperes that flows through it, that was formerly used as the unit of magnetomotive force.

○ An ampere-turn is represented by a steady, direct electric current of one ampere flowing in a single-turn loop of electrically conducting material in a vacuum.

○ The magnetomotive force is the force that produces the flux in the magnetic circuit, and the practical unit of magnetomotive force is the ampere-turn.

---

am|pli|fi|ca|tion /æmplɪfɪkeɪʃᵊn/

COMPUTING AND CONTROL

NOUN **Amplification** is the procedure of expanding the strength of a signal.

○ The nonlinear behavior of these components and their ability to control electron flows makes amplification of weak signals possible, and is usually applied to information and signal processing.

○ The amplification boosts weak signals, expanding your reception range and allowing you to receive more signals over a greater distance.

---

am|pli|fi|er (ABBR amp) /æmplɪfaɪər/ (amplifiers)

COMPUTING AND CONTROL

NOUN An **amplifier** is an electrical circuit that produces an output that is larger than the input.

○ An amplifier is a basic signal processing unit that increases the power of an audio signal.

○ As an amplifier simply magnifies what it is given, it will amplify the noise as well as the signal.

PRONUNCIATION

Note that in the nouns **amplifier** and **amplitude**, the main stress is on the first syllable. /<u>amp</u>-li-fi-er/ /<u>amp</u>-li-tude/

The noun **amplification** has two stressed syllables, with the main stress on the fourth syllable. /<u>amp</u>-li-fi-<u>ca</u>-tion/

---

am|pli|tude /æmplɪtud/

CIRCUITS / ELECTRICAL POWER

NOUN **Amplitude** is the maximum or peak value of a quantity or wave that varies in an oscillatory manner.

○ The oscilloscope is helpful in determining if the amplitude of the input waveform needs to be increased.

○ *In radio communications, a signal controls the amplitude of a carrier wave that is at a much higher, constant frequency.*

---

am|pli|tude mod|u|la|tion (ABBR **AM**) /ˈæmplɪtud mɒdʒəleɪʃᵊn/

COMMUNICATION: ANALOG

NOUN **Amplitude modulation** is a modulation method in which the carrier amplitude changes with the input signal amplitude.

○ *The broadcast of a single signal, such as a monophonic audio signal, can be done by straightforward amplitude modulation or frequency modulation.*

○ *In radio broadcasting amplitude modulation suffers more from atmospheric interference than frequency modulation.*

---

an|a|log (BRIT **analogue**) /ˈænᵊlɒg/

COMPUTING AND CONTROL

ADJECTIVE An **analog** system is a system in which an electrical value, such as voltage or current, represents something in the physical world.

○ *Analog circuits use a continuous range of voltage as opposed to discrete levels as in digital circuits.*

○ *Analog chips are needed to capture images and sound and translate them into digital information for transmission or storage.*

▶ COLLOCATIONS:
analog circuit
analog device
analog output
analog signal
analog system

US/UK ENGLISH

The spelling **analog** is usually used in American English.

The spelling **analogue** is usually used in British English.

an|a|log to dig|i|tal con|vert|er (ABBR **A/D converter**,

A to D converter; BRIT **analogue to digital converter**) /ænəlɒg
tə dɪdʒɪtəl kənvɜrtər/ (**analog to digital converters**)

COMPUTING AND CONTROL

NOUN An **analog to digital converter** is a device or circuit used to
convert an analog signal to a digital signal across a pair of terminals.

○ *The analog to digital converter inputs the analog pulse signal and outputs*
a digital output signal.

○ *The analog pulse signal is preferably amplified, shaped, and stretched to*
provide a stable analog pulse signal for the analog to digital converter.

AND gate /ænd geɪt/ (**AND gates**)

COMPUTING AND CONTROL: DIGITAL

NOUN An **AND gate** is an electrical circuit that combines two signals so
that the output is on if both signals are present.

○ *The output of the AND gate is connected to a base driver which is coupled to*
the bases of transistors, and alternately switches the transistors at opposite
corners of the inverter.

○ *An AND gate has two or more inputs and one output, and if the inputs applied*
to it are all 1, then the output will be 1.

an|gu|lar ve|loc|i|ty /æŋgyʊlər vəlɒsɪti/ (**angular velocities**)

CIRCUITS / ELECTRICAL POWER

NOUN **Angular velocity** is the rate of rotation about an axis, measuring
how the angle changes with time.

○ *Operation is smooth and quiet and, in the external rotor designs, the flywheel*
effect provides very uniform angular velocity.

○ *The work employed in getting the flywheel moving is stored in its angular*
momentum, and once it is moving, it wants to stay moving and resists
changes in its angular velocity.

an|ode /ænoʊd/ (**anodes**)

CIRCUITS

NOUN The **anode** of an electrical device is the positive electrode, which is
the element that receives the flow of electrons.

○ *Radio valves of the vacuum tube variety had anodes and cathodes through which current passed.*

○ *When a positive voltage is applied between the anode and cathode, current will flow through the diode, provided the voltage is greater than around 0.7V.*

RELATED WORDS

Compare **anode** with **cathode**, which is the negative electrode that provides the flow of electrons.

---

an|ten|na /æntɛnə/ (**antennas**)

COMMUNICATION

NOUN An **antenna** is a system of conductors that radiates and/or receives electromagnetic waves.

○ *A radio station pulses current through an antenna at the frequency it has been assigned, producing radio waves that propagate out from the antenna.*

○ *One of the unique functions of the meter is for tuning the transmitter for maximum power output and matching to the antenna.*

PRONUNCIATION

Note the irregular plural of this word and the way it is pronounced. **antennae** /æntɛni/

---

ap|par|ent pow|er /əpærənt pauər/

ELECTRICAL POWER

NOUN The **apparent power** of an alternating current circuit is the product of the RMS values of the voltage and the current, expressed as volt-amperes.

○ *The volt-ampere specification is used in AC circuits, but is less precise than in DC circuits, because it represents apparent power, which often differs from true power.*

○ *Power factor is best thought of intuitively as the multiplier (ranging between 0 and 1) that you must use to obtain the real power from the apparent power.*

ap|pli|ance /əplaɪəns/ (**appliances**)

ELECTRICAL POWER: POWER CONSUMPTION

NOUN An **appliance** is an item of equipment that uses current, and is not an electric light unit or an independent motor.

○ *For safety, a ground wire is often connected between the individual electrical appliances in the house and the main electric switchboard or fusebox.*

○ *These wire wound variable resistors are fitted in various circuits of electrical appliances and have the ability to withstand temperatures and varying voltages.*

a|rith|me|tic log|ic u|nit (ABBR **ALU**) /ærɪθmɛtɪk lɒdʒɪk yunɪt/ (**arithmetic logic units**)

COMPUTING AND CONTROL: DIGITAL

NOUN An **arithmetic logic unit** is a digital circuit used in computers to perform arithmetic and logic operations.

○ *The arithmetic logic unit may be used to perform multiplication as well as addition.*

○ *An 8-bit arithmetic logic unit would have to execute four instructions to add two 32-bit numbers, while a 32-bit ALU can do it in one instruction.*

ar|ma|ture /ɑrmətʃər/ (**armatures**)

ELECTRICAL POWER: MOTOR OR GENERATOR

NOUN The **armature** of an electric motor or generator or of an electric apparatus is the coil or coils in which a voltage is induced by a magnetic field.

○ *The motor has a flat armature, with coils mounted to face the rotor magnets.*

○ *In these generators, magnetic field which induces current in the armature coils is formed either by permanent magnets or electromagnets.*

ar|mored ca|ble (BRIT **armoured cable**) /ɑrmərd keɪbəl/ (**armored cables**)

ELECTRICAL POWER: DISTRIBUTION

NOUN An **armored cable** is a cable with a metal protective covering.

○ Armored cable assemblies are suitable for lashed aerial applications where corrugated steel tape protects the fiber optic cable from rodents and provides additional stiffness for aerial lashing.

○ There is an armored cable running from the ignition switch through the firewall, carrying the wire for the coil.

---

a|sym|met|ric dig|i|tal sub|scrib|er line (ABBR **ADSL**)
/ˌeɪsɪmɛtrɪk dɪdʒɪtᵊl səbskraɪbər laɪn/ (**asymmetric digital subscriber lines**)

COMMUNICATION: DIGITAL

NOUN An **asymmetric digital subscriber line** is a method for moving data over phone lines, carrying much more data than a modem can encode on a normal phone connection.

○ In an asymmetric digital subscriber line, the data throughput in the upstream direction, to the service provider, is lower, hence the designation of asymmetric service.

○ Demand for high bandwidth applications, such as video and file sharing, also contributed to popularize asymmetric digital subscriber line technology.

---

a|syn|chro|nous /eɪsɪŋkrənəs/

ELECTRICAL POWER: MOTOR OR GENERATOR

ADJECTIVE An **asynchronous** electric machine is one in which the magnetic field and the rotation are not exactly the same.

○ An asynchronous motor is an AC motor, usually an induction motor, whose speed slows with increasing torque to slightly less than synchronous speed.

○ Asynchronous machines do not operate at synchronous speed – their speed varies with the load.

▶ COLLOCATIONS:
asynchronous generator
asynchronous machine
asynchronous motor

---

at|ten|u|a|tion /ətɛnyueɪʃᵊn/

CIRCUITS / COMPUTING AND CONTROL

NOUN **Attenuation** is loss of signal power or amplitude caused during its transmission through a particular medium.

○ External attenuation involves placing a device between the amplifier and speaker, which reduces the amplifier's power and controls the overall volume level.

○ The strength of the signal will reduce because of the attenuation the circuit provides through losses.

WORD FAMILY

attenuation NOUN ○ Attenuation, or loss of signal strength, may occur as a result of physical barriers.

attenuator NOUN ○ An attenuator will reduce the amplitude of a signal.

Both of these come from the verb **attenuate**, which means "to reduce the strength of a signal."

---

at|ten|u|a|tor /ətɛnyueɪtər/ (attenuators)

COMPUTING AND CONTROL

NOUN An **attenuator** is a passive device used to reduce signal strength.

○ A power attenuator can be used to keep the desired tone, while reducing the speaker's volume level.

○ Another practical use of a power attenuator would be to reduce the power of an amplifier to match the power rating of the speaker.

---

au|di|o fre|quen|cy /ɔdioʊ frikwənsi/

COMMUNICATION: ANALOG

NOUN **Audio frequency** is a frequency that corresponds to audible sound waves, between 20 Hz and 20 kHz.

○ As volume level is decreased across the audio frequency band, the ear perceives the lows and highs to drop more than the mids.

○ The attenuation is almost constant over the whole audio frequency range.

au|to|mat|ic gain con|trol (ABBR **AGC**) /ɔtəmætɪk geɪn kəntroʊl/

COMPUTING AND CONTROL

NOUN **Automatic gain control** is a circuit that modulates an amplifier's gain, in response to the relative strength of the input signal, in order to maintain the output power.

○ *The effect of the automatic gain control is to reduce the gain and the signal level provided to a successive output buffer stage in order to improve the linearity of the overall amplifier chain.*

○ *Some telephone recording devices incorporate automatic gain control to produce acceptable-quality recordings.*

au|to|tim|er /ɔtoʊtaɪmər/ (**autotimers**)

GENERAL

NOUN An **autotimer** is a device for turning a system on and off automatically at times that have been set in advance.

○ *The autotimer circuit automatically turns off the amplifier when no signal is present.*

○ *At the end of the test period the autotimer closes its contact.*

au|to|trans|form|er /ɔtoʊtrænsfɔrmər/ (**autotransformers**)

ELECTRICAL POWER: TRANSFORMERS

NOUN An **autotransformer** is a transformer in which part of the winding is common to both primary and secondary circuits.

○ *These chargers use an autotransformer in which the primary and secondary windings are electrically connected.*

○ *Not all the power traveling from the primary to secondary winding of the autotransformer goes through the windings, so it can handle more power than a standard transformer, with the same windings.*

Bb

---

back E|M|F /bæk i ɛm ɛf/ (short for **back electromotive force**)

ELECTRICAL POWER: MOTOR OR GENERATOR

NOUN **Back EMF** is the system in the coil of an electric motor that opposes the current flowing through the coil, when the armature rotates.

- ○ When the speed varies, the winding characteristics may fluctuate, resulting in variation of back EMF.

- ○ At high speeds the traction motor armatures are rotating rapidly and have a high back EMF.

---

bal|anced three-phase /bælənst θrifeɪz/

ELECTRICAL POWER: DISTRIBUTION

ADJECTIVE A **balanced three-phase** voltage or current is one in which the size of each phase is the same, and the phase angles of the three phases differ from each other by 120 degrees.

- ○ A balanced three-phase network is one in which the impedances in the three phases are identical.

- ○ With such a balanced load, if a balanced three-phase supply is applied, the currents will also be balanced.

---

band|pass fil|ter /bændpæs fɪltər/ (**bandpass filters**)

COMPUTING AND CONTROL

NOUN A **bandpass filter** is a filter designed to pass all frequencies within a band of frequencies.

- ○ The bandpass filter offers two levels of selectivity, and its center frequency may be tuned from about 350 Hz to about 950 Hz.

- ○ The passband is the range of frequencies passed by an audio bandpass filter.

band|stop fil|ter /bændstɒp fɪltər/ (**bandstop filters**)

COMPUTING AND CONTROL

NOUN A **bandstop filter** is a filter designed to eliminate all frequencies within a band of frequencies.

○ A bandstop filter will allow high frequencies and low frequencies to pass through the filter, but will attenuate all frequencies that lie within a certain band.

○ The bandstop filter is used to reduce the reference sideband level.

band|width (ABBR **BW**) /bændwɪdθ/

COMMUNICATION

NOUN **Bandwidth** is the range of frequencies, or information, that a circuit can handle or the range of frequencies that a signal contains or occupies.

○ Bandwidth is the width of the range of frequencies that an electronic signal uses on a given transmission medium.

○ Since the frequency of a signal is measured in hertz, a given bandwidth is the difference in hertz between the highest frequency the signal uses and the lowest frequency it uses.

▶ COLLOCATIONS:
high bandwidth
low bandwidth

base load /beɪs loʊd/ (**base loads**)

ELECTRICAL POWER: DISTRIBUTION

NOUN The **base load** is the minimum load experienced by an electric system over a given period of time, that must be supplied at all times.

○ You might want to generate 2 or 3 kW at home from a high-efficiency fuel cell to meet your base load.

○ The system provides 100 kW of power, enough to meet the base load needs of 100 average homes or a small office building.

RELATED WORDS

Compare **base load** with **peak load**, which is the maximum load on an electrical power-supply system.

bat|ter|y /bætəri/ (batteries)

GENERAL

NOUN A **battery** is a device for turning chemical energy into electrical energy, consisting of a number of primary or secondary cells arranged in series or parallel.

○ *The battery cells are equipped with a filling port for distilled, demineralized water used to top up the free electrolyte.*

○ *Three rechargeable lead-acid batteries provide up to 15 hours of operation.*

> **TALKING ABOUT THE BATTERY**
>
> If you put electricity into a battery, you **charge** it or **recharge** it.
>
> If something uses all the electricity from a battery, it **drains** it.
>
> If you **disconnect** the battery, you stop it being connected to the electrical system.

bat|ter|y back|up /bætəri bækʌp/ (battery backups)

GENERAL

NOUN A **battery backup** is a system in some power supplies that switches between a main power source and a battery.

○ *Battery backup provides emergency lighting in the event of power failure.*

○ *The battery backup provides uninterrupted coupling of the gas turbine units to the power supply network.*

bi|di|rec|tion|al /baɪdɪrɛʃənᵊl/

CIRCUITS / COMMUNICATION

ADJECTIVE A **bidirectional** device accommodates signals traveling either direction though a single channel.

○ *Telephone lines are, by operational requirements, bidirectional.*

○ *Triodes for alternating current are bidirectional and so current can flow through them in either direction.*

> **WORD BUILDER**
> **bi-** = two
>
> The prefix **bi-** appears in several words meaning "two": **binary coded decimal**, **binary notation**, **bidirectional**.

bi|na|ry cod|ed dec|i|mal (ABBR **BCD**) /baɪnəri koʊdɪd dɛsɪməl/

| COMPUTING AND CONTROL: Digital |

ADJECTIVE A **binary coded decimal** number is one in which each decimal digit is encoded in binary, with four bits per decimal digit.

○ *Engineers do use binary coded decimal numbers for some operations, which use groups of four binary numbers to represent each digit of a decimal number.*

○ *Binary coded decimal code is formed by converting each digit of a decimal number individually into its binary form.*

bi|na|ry no|ta|tion /baɪnəri noʊteɪʃən/

| COMPUTING AND CONTROL: Digital |

NOUN **Binary notation** is a system of numbers that has only two different integer values 0 and 1.

○ *Each byte is comprised of four bits which, in binary notation, will describe adequately a number between 1 and 10 (the number 10 corresponding to the dialed zero).*

○ *Real numbers can also be represented using binary notation by interpreting digits past the decimal point as negative powers of two.*

bit /bɪt/ (**bits**)

| CIRCUITS / COMPUTING AND CONTROL |

NOUN A **bit** is the unit of information in information theory, consisting of the amount of information required to specify one of two alternatives 0 and 1.

○ *Bits are the basic unit of digital information.*

○ *A byte is eight binary digits, or bits.*

bit er|ror rate (ABBR **BER**) /bɪt ɛrər reɪt/ (**bit error rates**)

COMPUTING AND CONTROL: DIGITAL

NOUN A **bit error rate** is the measure of the number of incorrect bits that can be expected in a specified number of bits in a serial stream.

○ *In a digital communications system, a certain normalized signal-to-noise ratio would result in a certain bit error rate.*

○ *The probability of corruption for a single bit is called the bit error rate.*

black|out /blækaʊt/ (**blackouts**)

ELECTRICAL POWER: DISTRIBUTION

NOUN A **blackout** is a power loss affecting many electricity consumers over a large geographical area for a significant period of time.

○ *1,230 megawatts of demand response capacity helps to mitigate the risk of blackouts and reduce the cost of energy for all electricity users in the affected regions.*

○ *The system provides back-up power during times of blackout.*

block di|a|gram /blɒk daɪəgræm/ (**block diagrams**)

CIRCUITS / ELECTRICAL POWER / COMPUTING AND CONTROL

NOUN A **block diagram** is a diagram showing the interconnections between the parts of an industrial process.

○ *Figure 2 is a schematic block diagram illustrating a wireless communication device as a host device and an associated radio.*

○ *A detailed block diagram of an automatic gain control loop for use with a narrow band radio receiver is shown.*

Blue|tooth /bluːtuːθ/

COMMUNICATION: DIGITAL

NOUN **Bluetooth** is a technology that allows voice and data connections between a wide range of mobile and stationary devices through short-range digital two-way radio.

○ *Cellphone and PC manufacturers may enhance their Bluetooth product offerings with support for its low-energy wireless technology.*

○ *Bluetooth basically does the same thing a USB cable connection does, but it is a wireless connection to your printer, modem, and other peripherals.*

Bode plot /bəʊd plɒt/ (Bode plots)

INSTRUMENTATION, MEASURING, AND TESTING

NOUN A **Bode plot** is the graph of amplitude (in decibels) and phase against frequency (in logarithmic format). The Bode plot is named for US engineer Hendrik Bode (1905–1982).

○ *The straight line approximation of a Bode plot is easy to draw and gives reasonably accurate results.*

○ *The Bode plot shows that, in this case, high frequencies will not pass through the filter.*

Bool|e|an al|ge|bra /buːliən ældʒɪbrə/

CIRCUITS / COMPUTING AND CONTROL

NOUN **Boolean algebra** is a branch of symbolic logic used in computers.

○ *In Boolean algebra, logical operations are performed by operators such as "and", "or", in a similar way to mathematical signs.*

○ *These kinds of networks can be analyzed using Boolean algebra by assigning the two states, such as "on" / "off", to the Boolean constants "0" and "1".*

brake horse|pow|er (ABBR **bhp**) /breɪk hɔːspaʊər/

ELECTRICAL POWER

NOUN **Brake horsepower** is the horsepower of an engine measured by the degree of resistance offered by a brake, that represents the useful power that the machine can develop.

○ *For an electric motor, brake horsepower is the mechanical horsepower available at the shaft at specified rpm and full load current.*

○ *The difference between the brake horsepower and the indicated horsepower represents the rate at which energy is absorbed in overcoming mechanical friction of the moving parts of the engine.*

bread|board /brɛdbɔːd/ (breadboards)

GENERAL

NOUN A **breadboard** is an experimental arrangement of electronic circuits giving access to components so that modifications can be carried out easily.

○ *The test circuit is constructed on the breadboard as shown.*

○ *A breadboard, really an analog computer simulation, represents one specific combination of parts, each of which can vary widely creating virtually an infinite number of possible combinations.*

break|down /ˈbreɪkdaʊn/

CIRCUITS / ELECTRICAL POWER

NOUN **Breakdown** is the sudden transition from a high to a low dynamic resistance in a semiconductor device.

○ *Due to resonance, a very high voltage can develop across the secondary, until it is limited by some process such as electrical breakdown.*

○ *Breakdown is a rapid reduction in the resistance of an electrical insulator that can lead to a spark jumping around or through the insulator.*

breed|er re|ac|tor /ˈbriːdər riˈæktər/ (**breeder reactors**)

ELECTRICAL POWER: GENERATION

NOUN A **breeder reactor** is a nuclear reactor that produces the same kind of fissile material as it burns.

○ *The fast breeder reactor can generate all the electricity the world will need for thousands of years, but is highly dangerous, as it takes advantage of the plutonium buildup to generate new fuel.*

○ *A fast breeder reactor is a fast neutron reactor designed to breed fuel by producing more fissile material than it consumes.*

bridge rec|ti|fi|er /ˈbrɪdʒ ˈrɛktɪfaɪər/ (**bridge rectifiers**)

ELECTRONICS COMPONENTS

NOUN A **bridge rectifier** is a full wave rectifier consisting of a bridge with a similar rectifier in each of the four arms.

○ *A bridge rectifier will help to make sure that the current going to the DC path circuit is always at the correct polarity.*

○ *The two wire dimmer incorporates a full wave bridge rectifier so that the output of the dimmer is a rectified voltage.*

broad|band /brɔdbænd/

COMMUNICATION

NOUN **Broadband** is a transmission medium with enough bandwidth to carry multiple voice, video, or data channels at the same time.

○ *Our biggest concern about wireless broadband has stemmed from complaints about service reliability in areas of heavy foliage.*

○ *Electrical noise is generally broadband, which means it contains a wide spectrum of frequencies.*

brown|out /braʊnaʊt/ (brownouts)

ELECTRICAL POWER: DISTRIBUTION

NOUN A **brownout** is a situation in which the voltage supplied to a system falls below the specified operating range, but above 0V.

○ *When the compressor motor starts, it may introduce a voltage dip in the main power supply and cause a momentary brownout situation.*

○ *During peak loads there may be a brownout that causes voltage too low for some equipment to operate.*

bus /bʌs/ (buses)

COMPUTING AND CONTROL: DIGITAL

NOUN A **bus** is a data path that connects to a number of devices, such as that on a computer's circuit board or backplane.

○ *A bus acts as a shared highway and is in lieu of the many devoted connections it would take to hook every device to every other device.*

○ *A bus is an electrical connection component that can accept multiple cables or wires.*

bus|bar /bʌsbɑr/ (busbars)

ELECTRICAL POWER: DISTRIBUTION

NOUN A **busbar** is a rigid conductor used for connecting together several circuits.

○ *The system for monitoring partial discharge is connected in parallel with a busbar between a generator and an electric network.*

○ *A busbar is a metal strip in a distribution box that provides one connection point for all the circuits.*

by|pass ca|pac|i|tor /baɪpæs kəpæsɪtər/ (**bypass capacitors**)

ELECTRONICS COMPONENTS

NOUN A **bypass capacitor** is a capacitor that is placed between a direct current signal and ground to remove any alternating current component of the signal by creating an alternating current short circuit to ground.

○ *The bypass capacitor is used to bypass the power supply or other high-impedance component of a circuit.*

○ *The bypass capacitor presents a high impedance to the rectified AC input which results in the AC current being distributed symmetrically on the rising and falling edges of the rectified AC voltage.*

byte /baɪt/ (**bytes**)

CIRCUITS / COMPUTING AND CONTROL

NOUN A **byte** is a group of 8 bits.

○ *Combining bits into larger units called bytes creates more meaningful information.*

○ *A byte is eight binary digits, or bits.*

Cc

---

ca|ble /ˈkeɪbᵊl/ (cables)

GENERAL

NOUN A **cable** is a conducting wire or wires separated and surrounded by a dielectric substance or insulation.

○ In urban areas an underground cable is used to deliver power to buildings.

○ A transmission line is a cable for carrying an electrical signal from one place to another.

---

ca|ble trunk|ing /ˈkeɪbᵊl ˈtrʌŋkɪŋ/

GENERAL

NOUN **Cable trunking** is an enclosure usually with a rectangular cross section, and with one removable or hinged side, that is used to protect cables and provide space for other electrical equipment.

○ They make electrical ducting and cable trunking for concealing and securing cabling.

○ The cable trunking system will protect cables from dust or water ingress.

CAD /kæd/

GENERAL

ABBREVIATION **CAD** is the use of computer software in the design of electrical systems.

○ CAD is useful in drawing both mechanical and electrical layouts.

○ CAD is representational, static, geometric line drawings that have weight and dimension, their only data.

cal|o|rie (ABBR **cal**) /ˈkæləri/ (**calories**)

GENERAL

NOUN A **calorie** is the amount of heat required to raise the temperature of 1 gram of water through 1° centigrade.

○ Calories have largely been replaced in electrical calculations by the Joule which is 1 watt-second.

○ A current of 1 ampere maintained for 1 second in a 1-ohm resistor produces 0.239 calorie of heat.

ca|pac|i|tance /kəˈpæsɪtəns/

CIRCUITS / ELECTRICAL POWER / COMPUTING AND CONTROL

NOUN **Capacitance** is the ability of a system of electrical conductors and insulators to store electric charge when a potential difference exists between the conductors. The symbol for capacitance is C.

○ Capacitance is expressed as a ratio of the electrical charge stored to the voltage across the conductors.

○ Capacitance is a physical property of the capacitor and does not depend on circuit characteristics of voltage, current, and resistance.

ca|pac|i|tive cross|talk /kəˈpæsɪtɪv ˈkrɒstɔːk/

ELECTRONICS COMPONENTS

NOUN **Capacitive crosstalk** is a situation in which a signal on one line can cause a smaller version of the same signal on an adjacent line because of the capacitance between the lines.

○ Capacitive crosstalk occurs when there is interference resulting from the coupling of the electrostatic field of one conductor upon that of one or more other capacitors.

○ Capacitive crosstalk can sometimes be found in phone lines where one conversation is picked up on another line.

ca|pac|i|tor /kəˈpæsɪtər/ (**capacitors**)

CIRCUITS / ELECTRICAL POWER / COMPUTING AND CONTROL

NOUN A **capacitor** is a device consisting of two conducting surfaces separated by a layer of insulating material, that has the ability to store electric energy.

○ Even if you disable the device from the power supply some capacitors are able to store a charge for a long time.

○ The amount of charge that the capacitor can hold depends on the area of the two plates and the distance between them.

> **OTHER TYPES OF CAPACITOR INCLUDE:**
>
> bypass capacitor, coupling capacitor, electrolytic capacitor

ca|pac|i|ty /kəpæsɪti/

ELECTRICAL POWER: DISTRIBUTION

NOUN The **capacity** of a generating unit, generating station, or other electrical apparatus is the maximum load that it can carry.

○ Power transmission lines have enough capacity to carry very large currents.

○ The electricity system must have sufficient reserve capacity that the system can accommodate prolonged equipment shutdowns without significant interruption of electricity supply.

car|bon brush /kɑrbən brʌʃ/ (**carbon brushes**)

ELECTRICAL POWER: MOTOR OR GENERATOR

NOUN A **carbon brush** is a small block of carbon used to carry current between the stationary and moving parts of an electric generator or motor.

○ In a direct current motor a carbon brush is a device which conducts current between stationary wires and moving parts.

○ The carbon brush transfers the high voltage from the coil's secondary circuit to the distributor.

car|ri|er wave /kæriər weɪv/ (**carrier waves**)

COMMUNICATION

NOUN A **carrier wave** is the continuous electromagnetic radiation, of constant amplitude and frequency, that is given out by a transmitter.

○ The carrier wave is modulated in direct proportion to the signal, such as the voice or music, that is to be transmitted.

○ When information is broadcast from an AM radio station, the electrical image of the sound is used to modulate the amplitude of the carrier wave transmitted from the antenna of the radio station.

Ca|te|go|ry 5 (ABBR **Cat 5**) /kætɪgɔri faɪv/

COMPUTING AND CONTROL

ADJECTIVE The term **Category 5** refers to Ethernet cabling that allows data transfers up to 100 Megabits per second.

○ *The home control system operated over Category 5 network wiring, which made it simple to install and to maintain.*

○ *Category 5 cable is used for fast Ethernet and telephone communications.*

cath|ode /kæθoʊd/ (**cathodes**)

CIRCUITS

NOUN The **cathode** of an electrical device is the negative electrode, which is the element that provides the flow of electrons.

○ *The voltage would tend to build to dangerous levels across the coil unless we put a diode across the coil with the cathode on the negative end of the coil.*

○ *Fuel cells produce power electrochemically by passing a hydrogen-rich gas over an anode and air over a cathode, and introducing an electrolyte in between to enable exchange of ions.*

cath|ode ray os|cil|lo|scope (ABBR **CRO**) /kæθoʊd reɪ əsɪləskoʊp/ (**cathode ray oscilloscopes**)

INSTRUMENTATION, MEASURING, AND TESTING: INSTRUMENT

NOUN A **cathode ray oscilloscope** is an instrument based upon the cathode ray tube, that provides a visible image of one or more rapidly varying electrical quantities.

○ *A cathode ray oscilloscope may be used to display the variations in voltage signals.*

○ *A cathode ray oscilloscope is a tool for measuring variations in current from a source.*

cath|ode ray tube (ABBR **CRT**) /kæθoʊd reɪ tub/ (**cathode ray tubes**)

GENERAL

NOUN A **cathode ray tube** is a vacuum tube containing an electron gun and a fluorescent screen, that is used to display images.

○ *An electron gun is most often used in televisions and monitors which use cathode ray tube technology.*

○ *A cathode ray tube display will permit readout of more detailed information than at the workstations.*

Cel|si|us (ABBR **C**) /sɛlsiəs/

GENERAL

NOUN **Celsius** is an international scale for measuring temperature, in which water freezes at 0 degrees and boils at 100 degrees.

○ *Most programmable controllers are rated to operate from 0 to 60 degrees Celsius.*

○ *The extended operating temperature range of -40 to +125 degrees Celsius ensures these amplifiers can be used in extreme conditions, such as those found in industrial applications.*

---

charge /tʃɑrdʒ/ (**charges, charged, charging**)

GENERAL

VERB If you **charge** a battery, you pass an electrical current through it in order to make it more powerful or to make it last longer.

○ *A charge controller takes the energy from your solar panels and charges a battery.*

○ *Most small wind turbines are used for charging batteries, to provide a reliable stand-alone power source where grid power is not available.*

---

charge-cou|pled de|vice (ABBR **CCD**) /tʃɑrdʒ kʌpᵊld dɪvaɪs/ (**charge-coupled devices**)

SEMICONDUCTOR AND ELECTRONIC CIRCUITRY: DIGITAL

NOUN A **charge-coupled device** is one of the two main types of image sensors used in digital cameras.

○ *When a picture is taken, the charge-coupled device is struck by light coming through the camera's lens, and the pixels convert this light into movement of electrons.*

○ *A charge-coupled device is a device for the movement of electrical charge, usually from within the device to an area where the charge can be manipulated, for example, conversion into a digital value.*

chip /tʃɪp/ (**chips**)

ELECTRONICS COMPONENTS: DIGITAL

NOUN A **chip** is the finished integrated circuit.

○ *A microprocessor is a small chip part to control functions of a digital system like a music player, electronic calculator, or computer.*

○ *Memory modules are computer chips used to add memory to a computer.*

choke /tʃoʊk/ (**chokes**)

ELECTRONICS COMPONENTS

NOUN A **choke** is a coil of low resistance and high inductance that is used in electrical circuits to pass low frequency or direct currents while stopping the higher frequency alternating currents.

○ *Inductors called chokes are used as parts of filters in power supplies or to block alternating current signals from passing through a circuit.*

○ *Chokes are inductors used to eliminate alternating current above a certain frequency.*

C|H|P /si eɪtʃ pi/ (short for **combined heat and power**)

ELECTRICAL POWER: GENERATION

ABBREVIATION **CHP** is the production of both heat and electricity from the same device or power plant.

○ *By capturing the excess heat, CHP allows a more total use of energy than conventional generation, potentially reaching an efficiency of 70–90 percent.*

○ *A CHP product installed in a home and generating electricity at the point of use avoids these losses, capturing the heat for use in domestic hot water and heating in the home.*

cir|cuit /sɜrkɪt/ (**circuits**)

SEMICONDUCTOR AND ELECTRONIC CIRCUITRY

NOUN An electrical **circuit** is the complete path crossed by an electric current.

○ *When distributing three-phase electric power, a fourth or neutral cable is run in the street distribution to provide a complete circuit to each house.*

○ *An ampere is the unit of measurement of electrical current produced in a circuit by 1 volt acting through a resistance of 1 ohm.*

cir|cuit break|er (ABBR **breaker**) /sɜ́rkɪt breɪkər/ (**circuit breakers**)

ELECTRICAL POWER

NOUN A **circuit breaker** is a device that can stop the flow of electricity around a circuit by switching itself off if anything goes wrong.

○ *The circuit breaker works as a protection whenever electrical wiring in a building has too much current flowing through it.*

○ *A residual current circuit breaker cannot remove all risk of electric shock or fire.*

clock /klɒk/ (**clocks**)

CIRCUITS / COMPUTING AND CONTROL

NOUN A **clock** is the basic timing signal in a digital system.

○ *It is often assumed that a central processing unit with a higher clock speed will perform better, but although it is important, many other factors influence the performance of computers.*

○ *In order to conduct all of its designed operations, the CPU also has a clock which forms the basis for synchronizing the processor's actions with the remainder of the computer.*

cm /siː ɛm/ (short for **centimeter**)

GENERAL

ABBREVIATION A **cm** is a centimeter, which is 1/100 of a meter.

○ *At the top of the wire, a loop of about 6 cm in diameter has been made by folding the wire back on itself and soldering it in position before taping the joint with insulating tape.*

○ *Because the 2.4GHz wavelengths are so small, the antennas on the receivers do not need to exceed 3 to 5 cm.*

co|ax|i|al ca|ble (ABBR **coax cable**) /koʊǽlsiəl keɪbᵊl/ (**coaxial cables**)

CIRCUITS / COMMUNICATION

NOUN A **coaxial cable** is a way of transmitting electricity that usually consists of one central wire surrounded by an insulator and encased in either a wire mesh or a metal cover.

○ Each element that makes up the coaxial cable (conductor, dielectric, shield, and jacket) plays an important part in the performance, and needs to be carefully controlled in the manufacturing process.

○ Coaxial cable carries high-frequency or radio signals on a single conductor surrounded by an insulating material and contained within an outer conductor.

---

coil /kɔɪl/ (**coils**)

ELECTRICAL POWER

NOUN A **coil** consists of several loops of conductor that may be round a central ferrous core.

○ The coil used to be central to supplying high voltage to a car's sparking plugs.

○ An inductor is a circuit element consisting of a coil of wire wound on a core material made of ferrous or non-ferrous material.

---

com|mu|ta|tor /kɒmyəteɪtər/ (**commutators**)

ELECTRICAL POWER: MOTOR OR GENERATOR

NOUN A **commutator** is the metal cylinder or disk on the armature shaft of an electric motor, that is used to make electrical contact with the rotating coils and ensure that the current flows in a single direction.

○ The commutator switches power to the coils as the rotor turns, keeping the magnetic poles of the rotor from ever fully aligning with the magnetic poles of the stator field.

○ Motors run better when there is more contact area between the brushes and the commutator.

---

com|pact flu|o|res|cent lamp (ABBR **CFL**) /kɒmpækt flʊrɛsənt læmp/ (**compact fluorescent lamps**)

GENERAL

NOUN A **compact fluorescent lamp** is a small fluorescent lamp (= a tubular light bulb coated with phosphor which produces a bright light) that has a lamp life that is much longer than incandescent lamps.

○ A compact fluorescent lamp is a type of fluorescent lamp designed to replace an incandescent lamp.

○ In the United States, a compact fluorescent lamp can save over $30 in electricity costs over the lamp's lifetime compared to an incandescent lamp.

com|plex num|ber /ˈkɒmplɛks ˈnʌmbər/ (**complex numbers**)

CIRCUITS / COMPUTING AND CONTROL

NOUN A **complex number** is a number that is handled in 2 dimensions at the same time, as opposed to the single dimension for simple numbers.

○ We can't combine the two parts of the complex number because they represent different things, the real part and the imaginary part.

○ Unlike electrical resistance, the impedance of an electric circuit can be a complex number, but the same unit, the ohm, is used for both quantities.

con|duct|ance /kənˈdʌktəns/

CIRCUITS / ELECTRICAL POWER

NOUN **Conductance** is a measure of how easy it is for a particular voltage to force a current through a resistor.

○ The conductance value is one way to measure the resistive characteristic of any battery or cell.

○ Conductance is also sometimes referred to as "admittance" or "acceptance", because it relates the electrical or conductive efficiency of a circuit.

WORD FAMILY

conductivity NOUN ○ The conductivity of a material is affected by temperature.

conductor NOUN ○ Silver is a good conductor.

The noun "conductance" and both of the nouns above come from the verb **conduct**, which means "to enable electricity or heat to move through."

---

con|duc|tiv|i|ty /ˌkɒndʌkˈtɪvɪti/

CIRCUITS / ELECTRICAL POWER

NOUN Electrical **conductivity** is a measure of how easy it is for a current to be passed through a material.

○ The higher the conductivity of the material, the more current will pass for a given voltage.

○ Gold has a higher conductivity than copper and is often used to coat contacts because of this property.

con|duc|tor /kəndʌktər/ (**conductors**)

CIRCUITS / ELECTRICAL POWER / COMPUTING AND CONTROL

NOUN A **conductor** is a wire, cable, rod, tube, or bus bar designed for electrical current to pass.

○ When a direct current supply is connected to the conductor, it is seen to move.

○ When we get shocked we are usually in contact with the ground, an appliance or fixture, or something else that makes a good return conductor.

con|duc|tor loss /kəndʌktər lɔs/

CIRCUITS / ELECTRICAL POWER

NOUN **Conductor loss** is loss occurring in a conductor due to the flow of current.

○ Electromagnetic fields from the alternating currents produce voltages across conductors, causing eddy currents to flow in them, which increases the conductor loss and operating temperature.

○ Most power losses will be noted as an increase in heat in the specified material, and larger diameter conductors will provide less conductor loss.

con|duit /kɒndwɪt/ (**conduits**)

GENERAL

NOUN A **conduit** is a tube through which power or data cables pass.

○ Today almost 100 percent of wiring done in buildings is concealed, which increases the need for strong and safe conduits.

○ In an underground cable installation, heat conduction occurs everywhere except in the air space in the conduit.

con|nect|or /kənɛktər/ (**connectors**)

GENERAL

NOUN A **connector** is the part on a cable or an appliance that has female contact pins and is intended to be attached to the end of the flexible cable remote from the supply.

○ The USB connector allows you to charge and power your iPod, or any other USB powered product.

○ The low voltage bus is equipped with flexible connectors to the core and coil assembly to reduce transmission of vibration to the connected equipment.

con|sum|er u|nit /kənsuːmər yuːnɪt/ (**consumer units**)

ELECTRICAL POWER: POWER CONSUMPTION

NOUN A **consumer unit** is a particular type of distribution board that controls and distributes electrical energy, especially in domestic premises.

○ *Modern consumer units have ground leakage trips rather than fuses as protection.*

○ *A consumer unit normally has a single horizontal row of fuses or miniature circuit breakers.*

---

con|tac|tor /kɒntæktər/ (**contactors**)

ELECTRICAL POWER

NOUN A **contactor** is an electro-mechanical device that is operated by an electric coil and allows automatic or remote operation to start or stop an electrical power circuit.

○ *A contactor is a device for opening and closing an electric power circuit.*

○ *Large electrical currents are controlled by special-purpose relays called contactors.*

---

con|trol|ler /kəntroʊlər/ (**controllers**)

COMPUTING AND CONTROL

NOUN A **controller** is a piece of equipment that controls the operation of an electrical device.

○ *An adjustable speed drive might consist of an electric motor and controller that is used to adjust the motor's operating speed.*

○ *The counter determines how often the motor controller will move the stepper motor one step, thus setting the rate of stepping commands which, in turn, controls motor speed.*

---

con|vo|lu|tion /kɒnvəluːʃən/

COMMUNICATION: ANALOG

NOUN **Convolution** is a mathematical process used to characterize physical systems, similar to multiplication, but much more complex.

○ *Convolution is an important process used in physics and engineering, for example in digital image processing.*

○ *An out-of-focus photograph is the convolution of the sharp image with the shape of the iris diaphragm.*

cop|per loss /kɒpər lɔs/

CIRCUITS / ELECTRICAL POWER

NOUN **Copper loss** is loss occurring in a conductor due to the flow of current, when conductors were traditionally made of copper.

○ *In practice, energy is dissipated due both to the resistance of the windings (known as copper loss), and to magnetic effects primarily attributable to the core (known as iron loss).*

○ *The inductance will not significantly change due to larger wire, so you can use the same number of turns as you have now with heavier wire and it will reduce the copper loss.*

core loss /kɔr lɔs/

ELECTRICAL POWER: GENERATION

NOUN **Core loss** is the loss that occurs in a magnetic core due to alternating magnetization, which is the sum of the hysteresis loss and the eddy current loss.

○ *Higher-frequency harmonic currents cause increased core loss due to eddy currents and hysteresis, resulting in more heating than would occur at the same 60 Hz current.*

○ *The term core loss relates to the total energy lost through the generation of heat.*

co|ro|na dis|charge /kərouʲnə dɪstʃardʒ/

ELECTRICAL POWER

NOUN **Corona discharge** is a bluish white luminous discharge that appears surrounding a conductor surface and is not sufficient to cause sparking or flashover.

○ *Corona discharge is an electrical discharge brought on by the ionization of a fluid surrounding a conductor, which occurs when the strength of the electric field exceeds a certain value.*

○ *If the field is nonuniform, an increase in voltage will cause a corona discharge in the gas to appear at points with highest electric field intensity, which can be observed as a bluish luminescence.*

C

cor|ro|sion /kərouʒᵊn/

GENERAL

NOUN **Corrosion** is surface chemical action that occurs, especially on metals, by the action of moisture, air, or chemicals.

○ *Any electrical burns or corrosion on the contact point suggest the bulb is damaged or does not function properly.*

○ *Traditional contact-type power couplings, such as plug-and-socket connectors, are highly susceptible to corrosion when exposed to seawater.*

cou|lomb (ABBR C) /kulɒm/ (**coulombs**)

CIRCUITS / ELECTRICAL POWER

NOUN A **coulomb** is a unit of electric charge that is equal to the amount of charge accumulated in one second by a current of one ampere.

○ *An ampere is defined as a flow of one coulomb of charge in one second past some point.*

○ *A capacitance of one farad means that one coulomb of charge on each conductor causes a voltage of one volt across the device.*

> **WORD ORIGINS**
>
> This word is named for the French military engineer **Charles-Augustin de Coulomb** (1736–1806).

cou|pling ca|pac|i|tor /kʌplɪŋ kəpæsɪtər/ (**coupling capacitors**)

ELECTRONICS COMPONENTS

NOUN A **coupling capacitor** is a capacitor that is used to transmit an alternating current signal from one node to another.

○ *To preserve the values of voltage, current, and resistance within each stage, the coupling capacitor allows the AC variations to be coupled from an input source but blocks any DC coupling.*

○ *In analog circuits, a coupling capacitor is used to connect two circuits such that only the AC signal from the first circuit can pass through to the next while DC is blocked.*

cou|pling co|ef|fi|cient /kʌplɪŋ koʊɪfɪʃənt/ (**coupling coefficients**)

SEMICONDUCTOR AND ELECTRONIC CIRCUITRY

NOUN The **coupling coefficient** of a pair of coils is a measure of the magnetic effect passing between them.

○ It is important for a balancer coil for cold-cathode fluorescent lamps to have a high coupling coefficient between coils.

○ The balancer coil has to be layer-wound so as not to decrease the coupling coefficient.

C|P|U /si̱ pi yu̱/ (short for **central processing unit**)

COMPUTING AND CONTROL: DIGITAL

ABBREVIATION The **CPU** is the part of a computer that controls and carries out instructions or operations.

○ Today's computers (even the most powerful supercomputers) rely on CPUs that may be no larger than a postage stamp.

○ Since every computer needs to be able to do simple functions such as to add, to subtract, and to perform basic logical operations such as AND/OR, these are always included in a CPU.

cur|rent /kɜrənt/ (**currents**)

CIRCUITS / ELECTRICAL POWER / COMPUTING AND CONTROL

NOUN **Current** is the flow of electrons in a circuit. The symbol I is used for current, because current used to be referred to as electrical intensity.

○ When too much current passes through a fuse or breaker it blows, interrupting the flow of electricity.

○ The measure of the number of electrons flowing past a given point in an electrical conductor in a given amount of time is the electrical current.

cur|rent rat|ing /kɜrənt reɪtɪŋ/

CIRCUITS / ELECTRICAL POWER

NOUN **Current rating** is the maximum current that a fuse will carry for an indefinite period without too much deterioration of the fuse element.

○ A wide range of power switching transistors are also available, with current rating up to several hundred amperes and voltage ratings well over 1000V.

○ The higher the output current rating, the more power will be able to be supplied.

cur|rent source /kɜrənt sɔrs/ (current sources)

SEMICONDUCTOR AND ELECTRONIC CIRCUITRY

NOUN A **current source** is a source that maintains the current at a particular value almost independent of the load conditions.

○ The current source is a simple circuit, which will provide a current which remains constant regardless of the load placed at its output.

○ When there is no input signal, the output transistor's current must exactly equal the output of the current source.

cur|rent trans|form|er /kɜrənt trænsfɔrmər/ (current transformers)

INSTRUMENTATION, MEASURING, AND TESTING: DEVICES

NOUN A **current transformer** is a transformer that is designed to give an accurate current ratio for the purpose of measurement and control.

○ The most common type of alternating current transformer is one intended to transform a small electric current produced by a large electromotive force into a larger current of low electromotive force.

○ A current transformer can step down the current for a low current meter to monitor the high current circuit.

Dd

damp|ing /dæmpɪŋ/

CIRCUITS / ELECTRICAL POWER / COMPUTING AND CONTROL

NOUN **Damping** is the decrease in the amplitude of an oscillation or wave motion with time.

○ Resonance is the increase of amplitude as damping decreases and frequency approaches resonant frequency of a damped simple harmonic oscillator.

○ Damping devices are used on overhead power transmission lines to prevent conductor damage due to vibration induced by shedding of wind.

da|ta /deɪtə/

CIRCUITS / COMPUTING AND CONTROL

NOUN **Data** is information presented in numbers, letters, or other form.

○ System level soft errors typically occur as the data is traveling to and from the RAM on the data bus but not within the RAM chips themselves.

○ Serial communication is the sending of data one bit at a time.

USAGE

In general English, the noun **data** is usually followed by a singular verb, but in technical English, it is often followed by a plural verb and the singular form of the noun is **datum**.

○ Data are still being collected on the subject.

○ It is this datum in particular that interests me.

D

da|ta ac|qui|si|tion sys|tem /deɪtə ækwɪzɪʃ°n sɪstəm/
(data acquisition systems)

COMPUTING AND CONTROL: DIGITAL

NOUN A **data acquisition system** is a system that acquires data, generally by digitizing analog channels and storing the data in digital form.

○ *Data acquisition systems can be standalone or married to a computer and can acquire multiple channels of data.*

○ *The electronic signals from the weather station are transmitted to the data acquisition system where they are interpreted and stored for collection on a periodic basis.*

da|ta pro|cess|ing e|quip|ment /deɪtə prɒsɛsɪŋ ɪkwɪpmənt/

COMPUTING AND CONTROL: DIGITAL

NOUN **Data processing equipment** is electrically operated equipment that accumulates, processes, and stores data.

○ *Integrated circuits are utilized in a large range of products, including everyday articles, such as watches, television sets, and automobiles, as well as sophisticated data processing equipment.*

○ *All data processing equipment is designed to perform one or more of the five basic operations of classifying, sorting, calculating, summarizing, and recording data.*

D|C po|ten|ti|om|e|ter /diː siː pətɛnʃɪɒmɪtər/
(DC potentiometers)

ELECTRONICS COMPONENTS

NOUN A **DC potentiometer** is a potentiometer in which the supply is a battery and the balance is under direct current conditions.

○ *The voltage generated by thermocouples can also be measured by using a DC potentiometer.*

○ *A DC potentiometer can measure voltage directly and measure resistance, current, power, and temperature indirectly.*

dec|ade /dɛkeɪd/ (decades)

CIRCUITS / COMMUNICATION

NOUN A **decade** is a factor of 10 difference between two numbers.

○ *A decade is a range increasing by a factor of 10, such as 0.1–1, 1–10, and 10–100.*

○ *A decade is a range of frequencies for which the ratio of the highest frequency to the lowest is 10.*

dec|i|bel (ABBR **dB**) /dɛsɪbɛl/ (decibels)

CIRCUITS / COMPUTING AND CONTROL

NOUN A **decibel** is a method for specifying the ratio of two signals.

○ *The sound level on a microphone is measured in units of decibels relative to the average response of the system to all frequencies.*

○ *Generally speaking, through air, noise decreases by six decibels for a doubling of distance when sound emanates from a single point in space.*

del|ta con|nec|tion /dɛltə kənɛkʃ°n/ (delta connections)

ELECTRICAL POWER

NOUN A **delta connection** is a connection used in a three-phase electrical system in which three elements in series form a triangle, the supply being input and output at the three junctions.

○ *In the US, which uses mostly single-phase transformers, three identical single-phase transformers are often wired in a transformer bank in a delta connection, to create a three-phase transformer.*

○ *The delta connection consists of three-phase windings connected end-to-end which are 120° apart from each other electrically.*

de|mand /dɪmænd/

ELECTRICAL POWER: DISTRIBUTION

NOUN **Demand** is the rate at which electric energy is delivered to or by a system, part of a system, or a piece of equipment.

○ *Should the wind turbine produce more power than the demand of the house, this excess power is fed into the grid via a meter which counts the units fed in.*

○ *Reserve capacity is extra generating capacity available to meet peak or abnormally high demands for power and to generate power during scheduled or unscheduled outages.*

TALKING ABOUT DEMAND

If there starts to be more demand, you can say that demand **goes up**, **grows**, **increases**, or **rises**.

If there starts to be less demand, you can say that demand **declines**, **dwindles**, **falls**, or **goes down**.

---

de|mod|u|la|tion /dimɒdʒəleɪʃⁿn/

COMMUNICATION: ANALOG

NOUN **Demodulation** is the process of separating information from a modulated carrier wave.

○ *To perform the demodulation, an internal counter is used to determine the frequency of the incoming signal.*

○ *The output section demodulates the signal, restores it to the original analog input equivalent, and filters the ripple component, which resulted from the demodulation process.*

WORD BUILDER
-ation = the process of

The suffix **-ation** often changes a verb into a noun, meaning the "process of doing something:" **amplification**, **generation**, **modulation**.

---

de|tec|tor /dɪtɛktər/ (**detectors**)

SEMICONDUCTOR AND ELECTRONIC CIRCUITRY

NOUN A **detector** is an instrument to detect the unbalance in a bridge circuit.

○ *The further down the chain toward the output that a detector is placed, the more effect the non-linear distortion will have on the detection function.*

○ *The circuit acts as a phase detector by comparing the frequency of an oscillator with an incoming signal and then feeding back the output to keep the oscillator in phase with the incoming frequency.*

de|vice /dɪvaɪs/ (devices)

GENERAL

NOUN A **device** is an object that has been invented for a particular purpose, such as recording or measuring something.

○ If a miswiring inside an appliance caused one wire to accidentally touch the metal case of the device, your customers could still touch that metal case without danger.

○ A current transformer is a device for measuring a current flowing through a power system and inputting the measured current to a protective relay system.

di|e|lec|tric /daɪɪlɛktrɪk/ (dielectrics)

SEMICONDUCTOR AND ELECTRONIC CIRCUITRY

NOUN A **dielectric** is a non-conductor of electricity, or an insulator.

○ A dielectric is a substance in which an electric field gives rise to no net flow of electric charge but only to a displacement of charge.

○ The type of dielectric used between the plates of a capacitor will alter the capacitance of the capacitor.

di|e|lec|tric con|stant /daɪɪlɛktrɪk kɒnstənt/ (dielectric constants)

SEMICONDUCTOR AND ELECTRONIC CIRCUITRY

NOUN **Dielectric constant** is the ratio of the capacitance of a capacitor with the given material as dielectric, to the capacitance of the same capacitor with vacuum (or air) as the dielectric.

○ Substances with a low dielectric constant include a perfect vacuum, dry air, and most pure, dry gases such as helium and nitrogen.

○ The dielectric constant of a vacuum is defined as 1, that of air is very close to 1, and all other materials have values specified in relation to air or a vacuum.

di|e|lec|tric heat|ing /daɪɪlɛktrɪk hiːtɪŋ/

SEMICONDUCTOR AND ELECTRONIC CIRCUITRY

NOUN **Dielectric heating** is a form of heating in which electrically insulating material is heated by being subjected to an alternating electric field.

○ *A cellphone cannot cook anything; even a hundred cellphones put together could not cause the dielectric heating effect that you witness in a microwave.*

○ *Dielectric heating is most widely observable in the microwave oven where it operates most efficiently on liquid water, and much less so on fats, sugars, and frozen water.*

D

> **RELATED WORDS**
>
> Compare **dielectric heating** with **induction heating**, which is the heating of a conducting material as a result of the electric currents induced in it by an externally applied alternating magnetic field.

---

di|e|lec|tric loss /daɪɪlɛktrɪk lɔs/

SEMICONDUCTOR AND ELECTRONIC CIRCUITRY

NOUN **Dielectric loss** is the loss occurring in the leakage resistance of the dielectric.

○ *Normal ageing of an insulating material will also cause dielectric loss to increase.*

○ *If the cable is too small, the dielectric loss becomes large, resulting in overheating of the cable.*

---

di|e|lec|tric strength /daɪɪlɛktrɪk strɛŋkθ/

SEMICONDUCTOR AND ELECTRONIC CIRCUITRY

NOUN **Dielectric strength** is the ability of a dielectric material of specified thickness to withstand high voltages without breaking down.

○ *An oil should be heated before use, and tested for dielectric strength by observing the voltage required to create a spark between metal balls immersed in it at a distance of 1 mm apart.*

○ *The ground wires are suspended on insulators, the dielectric strength of which should be sufficient for the line operational conditions.*

---

dif|fer|ence am|pli|fi|er /dɪfərəns æmplɪfaɪər/ (**difference amplifiers**)

INSTRUMENTATION, MEASURING, AND TESTING

NOUN A **difference amplifier** is a device that amplifies the difference between two inputs, rejecting any signals common to both.

○ *The negative feedback into the difference amplifier allows the amplifier to compare the input to the actual output.*

○ *The operational amplifier is used as a difference amplifier, resulting in an output voltage equal to the difference of the latter two signals.*

---

di|gi|tal /dɪdʒɪtᵊl/

COMPUTING AND CONTROL

ADJECTIVE A **digital** system is one that operates using ones and zeros rather than analog signals.

○ *The digital computer is a device which has transformed the world in a very short time.*

○ *A digital circuit is based on a number of discrete voltage levels, as distinct from an analog circuit that uses continuous voltages to represent variables directly.*

▶ **COLLOCATIONS:**
digital circuit
digital device
digital output
digital signal
digital system

---

di|gi|tal me|ter /dɪdʒɪtᵊl mitər/ (**digital meters**)

CIRCUITS / ELECTRICAL POWER / COMPUTING AND CONTROL

NOUN A **digital meter** is a meter that gives a separate reading, in the form of a decimal number, for each given input quantity.

○ *A digital meter is one that displays values as numerical values rather than as the position of a meter on a relative scale.*

○ *An analog meter has a needle in it and reads like a gas gauge in a car, while a digital meter detects really low voltage and is more precise.*

---

di|gi|tal to an|a|log con|vert|er (ABBR **D/A converter**, **D to A converter**; BRIT **digital to analogue converter**) /dɪdʒɪtᵊl tu ænəlɔg kənvɜrtər/ (**digital to analog converters**)

COMPUTING AND CONTROL: DIGITAL

NOUN A **digital to analog converter** is a device or circuit that receives digital data as a stream of numbers and outputs a voltage or current proportional to the value of this digital data.

○ *Calculated digital samples are converted to voltages with a digital to analog converter.*

○ *The digital to analog converter converts the digital signal provided by the microcontroller to an analog voltage signal.*

---

di|ode /daɪoʊd/ (diodes)

ELECTRONICS COMPONENTS

NOUN A **diode** is a semiconductor device used in circuits for converting alternating current to direct current.

○ *A diode is a two-wire device that allows current to flow easily in only one direction.*

○ *The diodes are arranged to rectify the AC power from the line filter and to provide DC power across filter capacitor.*

---

di|rect cur|rent (ABBR DC) /dɪrɛkt kɜrənt/

CIRCUITS / ELECTRICAL POWER / COMPUTING AND CONTROL

NOUN A **direct current** is an electric current that always flows in the same direction from positive to negative poles.

○ *In a large generator, electromagnets are made by circulating direct current through loops of wire wound around stacks of magnetic steel laminations.*

○ *In direct current, the electric charges flow always in the same direction, which distinguishes it from alternating current.*

> **RELATED WORDS**
>
> Compare **direct current** with **alternating current**, which is a continuous electric current that periodically reverses direction, usually using a sine wave.

---

dis|charge /dɪstʃardʒ/ (discharges)

CIRCUITS / ELECTRICAL POWER

NOUN Electrical **discharge** can occur by the release of the electric charge stored in a capacitor through an external circuit.

○ *The discharge path was formed when a conductive liquid seeped into the plug-socket assembly.*

○ Capacitors may also have built-in discharge resistors to dissipate stored energy to a safe level within a few seconds after power is removed.

dis|charge tube /dɪstʃɑrdʒ tub/ (**discharge tubes**)

GENERAL

NOUN A **discharge tube** is an electrical device in which current flow is by electrons and ions in an ionized gas, as in a fluorescent light or a neon tube.

○ A gas discharge tube is a sealed glass-enclosed device containing a special gas mixture trapped between two electrodes, which conducts electric current after becoming ionized by a high voltage spike.

○ A discharge tube is an arrangement of electrodes in a gas within an insulating, temperature-resistant envelope.

disk /dɪsk/ (**disks**)

COMPUTING AND CONTROL: DIGITAL

NOUN A **disk** is a memory device that uses a magnetic medium for the storage of information.

○ Its rewritable disk format also allows the player to save created tracks.

○ The program takes up 2.5 megabytes of disk space, and can be run on a standard personal computer.

dis|play /dɪspleɪ/ (**displays**)

INSTRUMENTATION, MEASURING, AND TESTING

NOUN A **display** is the visual representation of a signal on a screen.

○ Troubleshooting is faster with on-screen display of trends and captured events, even while background recording continues.

○ You can review the captured data on-screen, in color, and zoom on areas of interest and spread them out across the maximum useable width of the display.

dis|trib|ut|ed gen|er|a|tion /dɪstrɪbyutɪd dʒɛnəreɪʃᵊn/

ELECTRICAL POWER: GENERATION

NOUN A **distributed generation** system involves a person or company generating some of their power requirements in different ways, such as locally, or using renewable energy, in order to avoid taking it all from the grid.

- ○ Combined heat and power plants can take the strain off the electric grid as they act as distributed generation systems.
- ○ Distributed generation can reduce the requirement for large power stations.

dis|tri|bu|tion line /dɪstrɪbyuʃⁱn laɪn/ (**distribution lines**)

ELECTRICAL POWER: DISTRIBUTION

NOUN A **distribution line** is a line or system for distributing power from a transmission system to a consumer that operates at less than 69,000 volts.

- ○ When a voltage greater than 1 kilovolt and less than 40 kilovolt is used for a particular power line, the power line is typically referred to as a distribution line.
- ○ When a producer of electric power wants to connect to the electric grid, a connection can be made at either distribution line or transmission line level depending on the plant's capacity.

dis|tri|bu|tion sys|tem /dɪstrɪbyuʃⁱn sɪstəm/ (**distribution systems**)

ELECTRICAL POWER: DISTRIBUTION

NOUN The **distribution system** is the part of an electric system after the transmission system that is dedicated to delivering electric energy to an end user.

- ○ A drop in voltage levels results when demand for electricity exceeds the capacity of the distribution system.
- ○ The form, rating, and characteristics of unit substations and their transformers are determined by the design of the electrical distribution system.

D|M|M /diː ɛm ɛm/ (short for **digital multimeter**)

INSTRUMENTATION, MEASURING, AND TESTING: INSTRUMENT

ABBREVIATION A **DMM** is an electronic measuring instrument with a digital display.

- ○ A common way to measure resistance, continuity, and voltage for general electrical troubleshooting is using a DMM.
- ○ The current will be supplied by a constant DC power supply and is measured using a DMM.

dou|ble in|su|la|tion /dʌbəl ɪnsəleɪʃən/

ELECTRICAL POWER

NOUN **Double insulation** is insulation that consists of both basic insulation and supplementary insulation.

○ *Equipment such as hand-held domestic electric drilling machines has the additional safety precaution of double insulation.*

○ *The aluminum housing is intertwined with an injection molded inner nylon core to combine the durability of an all metal body tool with the double insulation advantages of a tool with plastic housing.*

dry /draɪ/

SEMICONDUCTOR AND ELECTRONIC CIRCUITRY

ADJECTIVE If a soldered electrical joint is **dry**, it is imperfect because the solder has not adhered to the metal, which reduces its conductance.

○ *Failure to start up could be caused by dry joints on the line drive transformer pins.*

○ *A dry joint is a soldered electrical joint of poor quality, that results in problems such as an intermittent signal, crackles, distortion, or inconsistent operation.*

du|al-band /duəlbænd/

COMMUNICATION

ADJECTIVE **Dual-band** appliances operate across two frequency bands.

○ *Dual-band wireless networking offers some advantages that single-band networking cannot.*

○ *Many dual-band routers will let you broadcast two network signals simultaneously.*

duct /dʌkt/ (**ducts**)

GENERAL

NOUN A **duct** is a channel or pipe carrying electric cable or wires.

○ *PVC cable is the most common type of cable used when smoke-retardant properties are not required, because a building's electrical system is run through metal ducts, and not open ceilings.*

○ *Unless otherwise stated, ducts and trenches necessary to accommodate cables and equipment will be provided by the building contractor.*

D

dum|my load /dʌmi loʊd/ (dummy loads)

CIRCUITS / ELECTRICAL POWER / COMPUTING AND CONTROL

NOUN A **dummy load** is a resistive component that absorbs all the output power of an electrical generator or radio transmitter in order to simulate working conditions so that a system can be tested.

○ *A dummy load is needed for controller testing, so you don't have to spin up (and possibly damage) a real motor when testing controller designs.*

○ *A dummy load, as the name implies, acts like a real load as far as the supplying equipment is concerned.*

D|V|B /di vi bi/ (short for **Digital Video Broadcast**)

COMMUNICATION

ABBREVIATION **DVB** is a name for digital TV.

○ *DVB has been deployed worldwide to provide higher-quality images and sound, and more programming choices than analog does.*

○ *DVB is being adopted as the standard for digital television in many countries.*

dy|na|mo /daɪnəmoʊ/ (dynamos)

ELECTRICAL POWER: MOTOR OR GENERATOR

NOUN A **dynamo** is a device for converting mechanical energy into electrical energy.

○ *In a dynamo, the mechanical energy of rotation is converted into electrical energy in the form of a current in the armature.*

○ *The regulation of a direct current system between dynamo and translating device depends solely upon the resistance of the circuit.*

Ee

ear|phone /ɪərfoʊn/ (earphones)

COMMUNICATION

NOUN **Earphones** are devices that are held close to or inserted into the ear, that convert electric currents into sound waves.

○ You can experience and enjoy the same good quality of audio all around your home and outdoors with all these earphones without disruption.

○ The system will work well with headphones or earphones with an impedance from 16 to 300 ohms.

ed|dy cur|rents /ɛdi kɜrənts/

ELECTRICAL POWER

NOUN **Eddy currents** are localized electric currents set up in metal parts not normally meant to carry currents, due to changes in electromagnetic fields.

○ Low-frequency inductors are constructed like transformers, with cores of electrical steel laminated to prevent eddy currents.

○ The efficiency of a transformer may decrease as the frequency increases due to eddy currents in the core material.

e|lec|tri|cal cir|cuit /ɪlɛktrɪkəl sɜrkɪt/ (electrical circuits)

SEMICONDUCTOR AND ELECTRONIC CIRCUITRY

NOUN An **electrical circuit** is a complete route that an electric current can flow around.

○ The main aim of this earth leakage protection device is to detect faulty earth currents and to act by cutting the electrical circuit.

○ In an electrical circuit a capacitor will block direct current and will pass alternating current.

e|lec|tric charge /ɪlɛktrɪk tʃɑːrdʒ/

CIRCUITS / ELECTRICAL POWER / COMPUTING AND CONTROL

NOUN **Electric charge** is an amount of electricity that is held in or carried by something.

○ *1 coulomb is the amount of electric charge carried by a current of 1 ampere flowing for 1 second.*

○ *The capacitance value of any capacitor is a measure of the amount of electric charge stored per unit of potential difference between the plates.*

e|lec|tric cur|rent /ɪlɛktrɪk kɜrənt/

CIRCUITS / ELECTRICAL POWER / COMPUTING AND CONTROL

NOUN An **electric current** is a flow of electricity through a wire or circuit.

○ *The fuse wire is a thin wire that gets hot as the electric current passes through it.*

○ *Alternating current is electric current that repeatedly changes polarity from negative to positive and back again.*

e|lec|tric field /ɪlɛktrɪk fiːld/ (**electric fields**)

CIRCUITS / ELECTRICAL POWER / COMPUTING AND CONTROL

NOUN The **electric field** is an area in which a force is exerted on a charged particle.

○ *Charging a metal sphere to a high voltage produces an electric field in all directions.*

○ *The electric field between the plates of a capacitor resists changes in applied voltage.*

e|lec|tric flux /ɪlɛktrɪk flʌks/

CIRCUITS / ELECTRICAL POWER

NOUN **Electric flux** is a measure of the electricity coming out from a charged surface.

○ *The force between positive and negative charges is often described in terms of an electric flux linking them, which is measured using coulombs.*

○ *Electric flux can be visualized by flux lines emanating from positive charges and terminating on negative charges.*

e|lec|tric flux den|si|ty /ɪlɛktrɪk flʌks dɛnsɪti/

CIRCUITS / ELECTRICAL POWER

NOUN **Electric flux density** is electric flux passing through a unit area perpendicular to the direction of the flux.

○ *Electric flux density is a measure of the strength of an electric field generated by a free electric charge, corresponding to the number of electric lines of force passing through a given area.*

○ *Electric flux density is the amount of flux passing through a defined area that is perpendicular to the direction of the flux.*

e|lec|tric|i|ty /ɪlɛktrɪsɪti/

GENERAL

NOUN **Electricity** is a form of energy that can be carried by wires and is used for heating, lighting, and to provide power for machines.

○ *Always turn off the electricity before performing any maintenance on electrical appliances.*

○ *Most buildings are connected into the mains supply and this network typically generates electricity in power stations and then distributes it to the end user through a network of lines.*

e|lec|tric light /ɪlɛktrɪk laɪt/ (**electric lights**)

GENERAL

NOUN An **electric light** is a light produced by the use of electricity.

○ *Electric light sources may be of the incandescent, fluorescent, gas discharge, or LED type.*

○ *A flicker is a variation of input voltage, either magnitude or frequency, sufficient in duration to allow visual observation of a change in electric light source intensity.*

e|lec|tric mo|tor /ɪlɛktrɪk moʊtər/ (**electric motors**)

ELECTRICAL POWER: MOTOR OR GENERATOR

NOUN An **electric motor** is a device for converting electrical energy into mechanical energy in the form of rotation.

○ *In an electric motor, the moving part is called the rotor and the stationary part is called the stator.*

○ *Almost all domestic vacuum cleaners utilize an AC series-wound electric motor to spin the fan that generates suction and airflow.*

---

e|lec|tric po|lar|i|za|tion /ɪlɛktrɪk p͟o͟ʊlərɪzeɪʃᵊn/

GENERAL

NOUN **Electric polarization** is the type of polarization of electricity that occurs in a dielectric.

○ *Ferroelectricity is a property of a material whereby it exhibits a spontaneous electric polarization, the direction of which can be switched by applying an external electric field.*

○ *Ferroelectric materials are ceramics that exhibit permanent electric polarization in the absence of an electric field.*

---

e|lec|tric shock /ɪlɛktrɪk ʃɒk/ (electric shocks)

GENERAL

NOUN An **electric shock** is a dangerous and painful physiological effect caused by the passing of an electric current through the body of a human or animal.

○ *The ground connection also means that the surrounding building is at the same voltage as the neutral point and prevents a person from receiving an electric shock from the appliance.*

○ *The ground wire of a three-wire power cord acts as a protective mechanism against electric shock hazards.*

---

e|lec|tric strength /ɪlɛktrɪk strɛŋkθ/

CIRCUITS / ELECTRICAL POWER / COMPUTING AND CONTROL

NOUN **Electric strength** is the maximum voltage that an insulating material can take, after which it loses its insulating properties.

○ *The value obtained for the electric strength will depend on the thickness of the insulating material and on the method and conditions of test.*

○ *The higher the electric strength, the more useful is the material as an insulator.*

---

e|lec|tric sys|tem /ɪlɛktrɪk sɪstəm/ (electric systems)

ELECTRICAL POWER: GENERATION

NOUN An **electric system** consists of all of the elements needed to distribute electrical power, including overhead and underground lines, poles, transformers, and other equipment.

○ The electric system in a small industrial unit will normally be powered by a three-phase supply.

○ A motor is an electric device that consumes electric energy to rotate a device in an electric system.

e|lec|trol|y|sis /ɪlɛktrɒlɪsɪs/

CIRCUITS / ELECTRICAL POWER

NOUN **Electrolysis** is electric current passing through an electrolyte, that produces chemical changes in it.

○ There was also no visible electrolysis in the cell in terms of gas bubbles or plate erosion, which meant that the resistance of the cell would stay constant.

○ Electrolysis is the decomposition of a liquid compound by the passage of electric current through it.

e|lec|tro|lyte /ɪlɛktrəlaɪt/ (**electrolytes**)

CIRCUITS / ELECTRICAL POWER / COMPUTING AND CONTROL

NOUN An **electrolyte** is a substance, usually a liquid, that electricity can pass through.

○ When two different metals are suspended in an electrolyte solution, it can be found that direct current flowing one way through the metals has less resistance than the other direction.

○ They produce power electrochemically by passing a hydrogen-rich gas over an anode and air over a cathode, and introducing an electrolyte in between to enable exchange of ions.

e|lec|tro|lyt|ic ca|pac|i|tor /ɪlɛktrəlɪtɪk kəpæsɪtər/ (**electrolytic capacitors**)

ELECTRONICS COMPONENTS

NOUN An **electrolytic capacitor** is an electrical capacitor with an electrolyte between the two plates.

○ An electrolytic capacitor is a type of capacitor that uses an electrolyte as one of its plates, to achieve a larger capacitance per unit volume than other types of capacitors.

○ Electrolytic capacitors are generally used in electronic equipment, and their greatest advantage is that they can exhibit a large amount of capacitance in a small case size.

e|lec|tro|mag|net /ɪlɛktroʊmægnɪt/ (**electromagnets**)

ELECTRICAL POWER

NOUN An **electromagnet** is a temporary magnet formed by winding a coil of wire round a piece of soft iron, and passing an electric current through it.

○ *The electricity magnetizes the electromagnet, and when the current jumps to unsafe levels, the electromagnet is strong enough to pull down a metal lever connected to the switch linkage.*

○ *The electromagnet provides the driving force to close the contacts, which are the current carrying part of the contactor.*

e|lec|tro|mag|net|ic /ɪlɛktroʊmægnɛtɪk/

CIRCUITS / COMMUNICATION

ADJECTIVE If something is described as **electromagnetic**, it has been made by, contains, or is operated by an electromagnet.

○ *Sun and fires are natural sources of electromagnetic radiation energy, and microwaves, radio transmission, lamps, and lasers are manufactured sources.*

○ *A radio wave is an electromagnetic wave propagated by an antenna.*

▶ COLLOCATIONS:
electromagnetic force
electromagnetic radiation
electromagnetic wave

e|lec|tro|mag|net|ic com|pat|i|bil|i|ty (ABBR **EMC**)
/ɪlɛktroʊmægnɛtɪk kəmpætɪbɪlɪti/

CIRCUITS / ELECTRICAL POWER / COMPUTING AND CONTROL

NOUN **Electromagnetic compatibility** is the ability of electronic equipment not to cause or react to electromagnetic interference from other electronic equipment.

○ *We have worked on this product to reduce or eliminate external magnetic fields to meet safety and electromagnetic compatibility requirements.*

○ *Products that fail to meet these specifications for electromagnetic compatibility cannot be branded with the CE mark for sale in the European community.*

e|lec|tro|mag|net|ic field /ɪlɛktroʊmægnɛtɪk fiːld/
(**electromagnetic fields**)

CIRCUITS / ELECTRICAL POWER

NOUN An **electromagnetic field** is an electric and magnetic force field that surrounds a moving electric charge.

○ *The motion of charges also creates an electromagnetic field around the conductor that exerts a mechanical radial squeezing force on the conductor.*

○ *The electromagnetic field is a physical field produced by electrically charged objects.*

e|lec|tro|mag|net|ic in|ter|fer|ence (ABBR **EMI**)
/ɪlɛktroʊmægnɛtɪk ɪntərfɪərəns/

GENERAL

NOUN **Electromagnetic interference** is unwanted noise or other effects from electromagnetic radiation.

○ *A 6-inch square solid copper busbar is just as susceptible to electromagnetic interference as a hair thickness wire.*

○ *As a means for preventing electromagnetic interference within an electronic apparatus, electronic components and circuits are covered with electromagnetic radiation shielding material.*

e|lec|tro|mag|net|ic spec|trum /ɪlɛktroʊmægnɛtɪk spɛktrəm/ (**electromagnetic spectra**)

GENERAL

NOUN An **electromagnetic spectrum** is the range of frequencies over which electromagnetic radiations are caused.

○ *The electromagnetic spectrum is a vast band of energy frequencies extending from radio waves to gamma waves, from the very lowest frequencies to the highest possible frequencies.*

○ *All of the frequencies we use for transmitting and receiving energy are part of the electromagnetic spectrum.*

e|lec|tro|me|chan|i|cal /ɪlɛktroʊmɪkænɪkᵊl/

GENERAL

ADJECTIVE An **electromechanical** device is an electrically operated mechanical device.

○ *Because modern receivers are purely electronic devices with no moving parts unlike electromechanical devices like turntables and cassette decks, they tend to offer many years of trouble-free service.*

○ *Electromechanical devices such as the generator on an automobile convert mechanical energy to direct current.*

e|lec|tro|mo|tive force (ABBR **EMF**) /ɪlɛktroʊmoʊtɪv fɔrs/

GENERAL

NOUN **Electromotive force** is voltage, or the difference in the electric tension or the difference in charge between two points that causes an electric current.

○ *The potential difference between two points of a conductor creates an electromotive force which pushes free electrons in a conducting material to move towards the positive terminal, creating current.*

○ *This varying magnetic field induces a varying electromotive force or "voltage" in the secondary winding.*

e|lec|tron /ɪlɛktrɒn/ (**electrons**)

CIRCUITS / ELECTRICAL POWER / COMPUTING AND CONTROL

NOUN An **electron** is an elementary particle that has a negative charge and is a constituent of all atoms.

○ *Electric current is the flow of electrons in an electrical conductor.*

○ *In North America, electricity is generated at 60 Hz, which means the electrons move forward, then back again, 60 times in one second.*

e|lec|tron gun /ɪlɛktrɒn gʌn/ (**electron guns**)

INSTRUMENTATION, MEASURING, AND TESTING

NOUN An **electron gun** is the source of electrons in a cathode ray tube.

○ *An electron gun consists of a cathode emitter of electrons, an anode with an aperture through which the beam of electrons can pass, and one or more focusing and control electrodes.*

○ *An electron gun is an electrical component that produces an electron beam that has a precise kinetic energy and is most often used in televisions and monitors which use cathode ray tube technology.*

e|lec|tron volt /ɪlɛktrɒn vəʊlt/ (**electron volts**)

CIRCUITS / ELECTRICAL POWER / COMPUTING AND CONTROL

NOUN An **electron volt** is the unit of energy used in dealing with subatomic particles, equal to the increase in energy or the work done on an electron when passing through a potential rise of 1 volt.

○ *A unit of energy in nuclear physics is the electron volt, which is defined as the energy gained by an electron in rising through a potential difference of one volt.*

○ *Because electron volts precisely measure such small quantities of energy, they rank as the unit of choice for nuclear and atomic physics.*

e|lec|tro|stat|ic /ɪlɛktrəʊstætɪk/

CIRCUITS / ELECTRICAL POWER / COMPUTING AND CONTROL

ADJECTIVE An **electrostatic** effect is an effect that relates to an electric field, or is created by an electric charge.

○ *As electrostatic effects are dependent upon the potential and frequency, to produce the most powerful action it is desirable to increase both as far as practicable.*

○ *Electrostatic lines of force are strongest when the charged particles that create them are close together.*

▶ **COLLOCATIONS:**
electrostatic charge
electrostatic discharge
electrostatic effect
electrostatic energy

en|er|gy /ɛnərdʒi/

CIRCUITS / ELECTRICAL POWER / COMPUTING AND CONTROL

NOUN Electrical **energy** is power from electricity, measured in joules, that makes machines work or produces heat.

○ *The battery stores the energy when the wind generation system is producing more power than is needed.*

○ *A generator is a machine that converts mechanical energy into electrical energy.*

en|gine /ˈɛndʒɪn/ (engines)

ELECTRICAL POWER: MOTOR OR GENERATOR

NOUN An **engine** is a device for converting one form of energy into another, especially for converting other forms of energy into mechanical energy.

○ Diesel or gas-fired engines are the principal types used in electric plants.

○ Recent technological developments that involve thermo-acoustic engines and converters hold the promise of converting up to 40 percent of high-grade thermal energy into electric power.

E|PROM /ˈiprɒm/ (EPROMs) (short for **erasable programmable read-only memory**)

COMPUTING AND CONTROL: DIGITAL

NOUN An **EPROM** is a type of memory chip that retains its data when its power supply is switched off.

○ In a typical microcomputer, a central processing unit executes an operating program stored in an EPROM which also stores tables and data utilized in the program.

○ The microcomputer also includes a RAM into which data may be temporarily stored and from which data may be read at various address locations determined by the program stored in the EPROM.

e|quip|ment /ɪkwɪpmənt/

GENERAL

NOUN Electrical **equipment** is material, fittings, devices, and appliances that are used as a part of, or in connection with, an electrical installation.

○ When using portable equipment, the risk of electric shock can be reduced by using a low voltage supply.

○ As with all electrical equipment, it is important to keep fuses and breakers from getting wet.

e|qui|po|ten|tial /ˌɛkwɪpətɛnʃᵊl/

CIRCUITS / ELECTRICAL POWER / COMPUTING AND CONTROL

ADJECTIVE **Equipotential** lines and surfaces have the same electric potential as each other.

○ *A conductor shielding is an envelope that encloses the conductor of a cable and provides an equipotential surface in contact with the cable insulation.*

○ *Between parallel plates, equipotential lines can be related to electric field strengths, because they evenly divide up the space between the plates, as does the field strength.*

E|S|D /i ɛs di/ (short for **electrostatic discharge**)

ELECTRICAL POWER

ABBREVIATION **ESD** is the release of stored static electricity, usually the potentially damaging discharge of many thousands of volts that occurs when an electronic device is touched by a charged body.

○ *Be sure to take the proper ESD precautions such as ground straps, gloves, mats, or other protective measures to avoid damaging the processor and other electrical components in the system.*

○ *ESD comes from the static charge accumulated on many different kinds of materials, which finds a return to ground or a mass that attracts the excess electrons.*

---

ex|cite /ɪksaɪt/ (**excites, excited, exciting**)

ELECTRICAL POWER: MOTOR OR GENERATOR

VERB If a current **excites** the coils of a generator or motor, it supplies electricity to them in order to create a magnetic field.

○ *This type of machine is excited with a concentrated winding located on each pole.*

○ *The shunt field windings of both DC machines are independently excited through variable resistors.*

---

ex|po|nent /ɛkspoʊnənt/ (**exponents**)

GENERAL

NOUN An **exponent** is the number indicating the power of a quantity.

○ *It is common to encounter very small and very large numbers in electronics, and the exponent indicates the number of decimal places to the right or left of the decimal point in the number.*

○ *An exponent is the number of places the decimal must be moved, so where the exponent of 10 is a positive number, move the decimal point to the right.*

Ff

far|ad (ABBR F) /fǽrəd/ (farads)

CIRCUITS / ELECTRICAL POWER / COMPUTING AND CONTROL

NOUN A **farad** is a unit of capacitance.

- ○ One coulomb can be defined as one farad of capacitance times one volt of electric potential difference.

- ○ Because the farad is a very large quantity, capacitance in electronic applications is usually expressed in millionths of a farad.

> **WORD ORIGINS**
>
> This word is named for **Michael Faraday** (1791–1867), the English physicist and chemist who contributed to the fields of electromagnetism and electrochemistry.

fault /fɔ̱lt/ (faults)

SEMICONDUCTOR AND ELECTRONIC CIRCUITRY

NOUN A **fault** in an electrical circuit, component, or line is a defect, such as a short circuit.

- ○ In the event of a fault, the ground wire can carry enough current to blow a fuse and isolate the faulty circuit.

- ○ If the equipment has a fault and the electricity is going along the ground wire, the chances are that too much current will flow through the fuse and so the fuse gets too hot and melts.

fault cur|rent /fɔ̱lt kɜ̱rənt/ (fault currents)

CIRCUITS / ELECTRICAL POWER

NOUN A **fault current** is a current that results from a fault.

○ It is the responsibility of the electrical contractor to know how much fault current is available at all points in the electrical system, and to select and install components capable of handling it.

○ Fault current calculations are needed in an electrical system to ensure that the system can safely handle and protect the specified equipment during a short circuit.

---

fault-tol|er|ant /fɔlt tɒlərənt/

CIRCUITS / ELECTRICAL POWER

ADJECTIVE A **fault-tolerant** electrical system will tolerate excessive voltage when there is a fault.

○ The fault-tolerant appliance design increases manufacturing up-time and saves replacement costs by as much as 75 percent.

○ We will need highly reliable, fault-tolerant, autonomously controlled electrical power systems to deliver high-quality power from the sources to the loads.

---

feed|back (ABBR FB) /fidbæk/

COMPUTING AND CONTROL

NOUN **Feedback** is the process of part of the signal coming out of a piece of electrical equipment going back into it to reduce or increase the amplification.

○ Negative feedback is used to stabilize a system by feeding back a proportion of the output to the input but in opposition to the input signal.

○ When a sound system howls because the microphone is too near the speaker, this is an example of positive feedback.

---

fer|ro|mag|net|ism /fɛroʊmægnɪtɪzəm/

GENERAL

NOUN **Ferromagnetism** is the magnetic force that materials like iron, nickel, or cobalt show when they are in a magnetic field.

○ Ferromagnetism is the ability of materials to be attracted to a magnet.

○ Ferromagnetism is primarily caused by unpaired electron magnetic moments.

F|E|T /ɛf i ti/ (short for **field-effect transistor**)

SEMICONDUCTOR AND ELECTRONIC CIRCUITRY

ABBREVIATION An **FET** is a transistor in which the voltage on one terminal creates a field that allows or disallows conduction between the other two terminals.

○ An FET is a transistor that uses an electric field to control the conductivity of a particular channel in a semiconductor material.

○ With an FET, the output current flowing between the source and drain terminals is controlled by a variable electric field applied to the gate terminal.

field /fild/ (**fields**)

CIRCUITS / ELECTRICAL POWER

NOUN An electric or magnetic **field** is the area in which an electrically charged body or a magnetized body has an effect.

○ The electricity entering the house runs through a pair of loops that induce a magnetic field.

○ The electric field set up inside the tube excites atoms of mercury gas, making them emit ultraviolet light.

field wind|ing /fild waindɪŋ/ (**field windings**)

ELECTRICAL POWER: MOTOR OR GENERATOR

NOUN A **field winding** is the insulated current-carrying coils on a field magnet that produce the magnetic field needed to excite a generator or motor.

○ As each coil is energized in turn, the rotor aligns itself with the magnetic field produced by the energized field winding.

○ It is essential that the field windings of the generator be excited with DC current.

fil|a|ment /filəmənt/ (**filaments**)

GENERAL

NOUN A **filament** is the thin wire inside a light bulb that emits light when heated by an electric current.

○ The incandescent light bulb makes light by heating a metal filament wire to a high temperature until it glows.

○ *If you close the switch for a fraction of a second, then open it for the same amount of time, the filament won't have time to cool down and heat up, and you will just get an average glow of 50W.*

flash|o|ver /flǽʃoʊvər/ (**flashovers**)

ELECTRICAL POWER: DISTRIBUTION

NOUN A **flashover** is an electric discharge over or around the surface of an insulator.

○ *When an electrical flashover occurs, conductors can vaporize, expanding to thousands of times their original volume.*

○ *In electric power transmission, a flashover is an unintended high voltage electric discharge over or around an insulator, or sparking between two or more adjacent conductors.*

flex /flɛks/ (**flexes**)

GENERAL

NOUN A **flex** is a flexible insulated electric cable, used especially to connect appliances to the mains electricity.

○ *Faulty flexes on electrical appliances cause 1,000 fires and several deaths a year.*

○ *Buy specially designed childproof safety covers to protect your child from open sockets and ensure that all electrical flexes are pushed to the back of work surfaces, well out of reach.*

flip flop /flɪp flɒp/ (**flip flops**)

COMPUTING AND CONTROL: DIGITAL

NOUN A **flip flop** is a memory device that is used in digital equipment to store a one or a zero as a bit of memory.

○ *A flip flop is a bistable multivibrator, which is capable of storing one bit of information.*

○ *The common hardware storage device is the flip flop.*

flux link|age /flʌks lɪŋkɪdʒ/

ELECTRICAL POWER

NOUN **Flux linkage** is the linking of the magnetic field with the conductors of a coil when the magnetic field passes through the loops of the coil, expressed as a value.

○ *The flux linkage of a coil is simply an alternative term for total flux, used for convenience in engineering applications.*

○ *Flux linkage can also be expressed as the time integral of the voltage over the winding and measured in volt seconds.*

Fou|ri|er a|nal|y|sis /fʊərɪeɪ ənælɪsɪs/ (**Fourier analyses**)

CIRCUITS / COMMUNICATION

NOUN **Fourier analysis** is the analysis of a periodic function into its simple sinusoidal or harmonic components, whose sum forms a Fourier series. Fourier analysis is named for French mathematician Joseph Fourier (1768–1830).

○ *The use of Fourier analysis simplifies the task of designing communication equipment.*

○ *Fourier analysis allows any signal to be constructed from a spectrum of frequencies, whence the circuit's reaction to the various frequencies may be found.*

Fou|ri|er se|ries /fʊərɪeɪ sɪəriz/ (**Fourier series**)

CIRCUITS / COMMUNICATION

NOUN A **Fourier series** is an infinite series of harmonic sinusoidal components used to represent a periodic function. The Fourier series is named for French mathematician Joseph Fourier (1768–1830).

○ *Each of the significant terms of the Fourier series can be used to test the response of the system to that term.*

○ *It can be shown that virtually all periodic functions of time can be represented by a Fourier series.*

Fou|ri|er trans|form (ABBR **FT**) /fʊərɪeɪ trænsfɔrm/ (**Fourier transforms**)

COMMUNICATION: ANALOG

NOUN A **Fourier transform** is a mathematical technique for converting a time function into one expressed in terms of frequency. The Fourier transform is named for French mathematician Joseph Fourier (1768–1830).

○ *In designing modern communication equipment, the benefit of the Fourier transform cannot be overstated.*

○ *A Fourier transform is a circuit analysis technique that decomposes or separates a waveform or function into sinusoids of different frequency which sum to the original waveform.*

fre|quen|cy /frɪ̱kwənsi/

CIRCUITS / ELECTRICAL POWER / COMPUTING AND CONTROL

NOUN Electrical **frequency** is the number of complete cycles of an alternating voltage or current in a particular amount of time, measured in hertz.

○ A radio station pulses current through an antenna at the frequency it has been assigned, producing radio waves that propagate out from the antenna.

○ When the tube lights, the voltage and frequency across the tube and capacitor typically both drop, thus capacitor current falls to a low but non-zero value.

fre|quen|cy mod|u|la|tion (ABBR **FM**) /frɪ̱kwənsi mɒdʒəleɪʃ°n/

COMMUNICATION: ANALOG

NOUN **Frequency modulation** is a process in which the frequency of the carrier is controlled by the modulating signal.

○ Frequency modulation is less error-prone than amplitude modulation as a broadcast means.

○ The broadcast of a single signal, such as a monophonic audio signal, can be done by straightforward amplitude modulation or frequency modulation.

fre|quen|cy re|sponse /frɪ̱kwənsi rɪspɒns/ (**frequency responses**)

COMPUTING AND CONTROL

NOUN The **frequency response** of a circuit is the way in which it varies voltage or current with change in frequency.

○ Carbon microphones have poor frequency response and bad signal-to-noise ratios, and they are only suitable for telephones and such communication applications.

○ Reducing the bandwidth of the circuit to a minimum will also minimize noise, and there is also a requirement to match the bandwidth to the frequency response required for the input signal.

fre|quen|cy spec|trum /frɪ̱kwənsi spɛktrəm/ (**frequency spectra**)

CIRCUITS / COMMUNICATION

NOUN The **frequency spectrum** of an electrical signal is the distribution of the amplitudes and phases of each frequency component against frequency.

○ The use of higher frequencies is desirable because of the smaller antenna size, the improved directional effect of the antennae, and the broader available frequency spectrum.

○ A full-range device is any audio device capable of capturing, reproducing, or processing the full audio frequency spectrum of 20 Hz to 20 kHz.

full load cur|rent /fʊl loʊd kɜrənt/

ELECTRICAL POWER: MOTOR OR GENERATOR

NOUN A **full load current** is the largest current that a motor or other device is designed to carry under particular conditions.

○ The starters shall be suitably rated to continuously carry the full load current of the motor and also accept the starting current surges without tripping.

○ Typically, the bypass contactor is much smaller than what is needed for a full voltage start as the contacts only need to be able to handle the full load current of the motor.

full wave rec|ti|fi|er /fʊl weɪv rɛktɪfaɪər/ (**full wave rectifiers**)

ELECTRICAL POWER

NOUN A **full wave rectifier** is a device that converts an alternating signal, with positive and negative signal components, to one in which all parts of the signal are positive.

○ For single-phase AC, if the transformer is center-tapped, then two diodes back-to-back, anodes-to-anode or cathode-to-cathode, form a full wave rectifier.

○ A full wave rectifier is an efficient mechanism for converting alternating current into direct current.

fuse /fyuz/ (**fuses**)

GENERAL

NOUN A **fuse** is a protective device in an electric plug or circuit that contains a piece of wire designed to melt and break when there is a fault, and an excessive current flows along it for a particular time.

○ Fuses help protect your electronic equipment, and without them, any stray electrical surge – from lightning, large appliances, or the electric provider – could destroy your equipment.

○ A fuse or a circuit breaker is normally used as a disconnector.

Gg

gain /geɪn/ (gains)

ELECTRICAL POWER: Generation

NOUN **Gain** is the amount of amplification that an amplifier circuit produces.

○ A gain of 2 would mean that the output is scaled to twice the amplitude of the input.

○ Decibels are units used to express power gain in amplifiers or power loss in passive circuits or cables.

gen|er|ate /dʒɛnəreɪt/ (generates, generated, generating)

ELECTRICAL POWER: GENERATION

VERB If a system **generates** electricity, it produces it, especially in a power station.

○ The utility company will generate, transmit, and distribute supplies of electric energy to a specified area not being serviced by another utility.

○ The network generates electricity in power stations and then distributes it to the end user through a network of overhead and underground lines.

gen|er|a|tion /dʒɛnəreɪʃən/

ELECTRICAL POWER: GENERATION

NOUN **Generation** of electricity is the process of producing electrical energy by transforming non electrical forms of energy.

○ Wind generators are ideal since they produce maximum power during a monsoon when solar power generation is minimum.

○ A wave farm or wave power farm is a collection of machines in the same location and used for the generation of wave power electricity.

gen|er|a|tor /dʒɛnəreɪtər/ (generators)

ELECTRICAL POWER: GENERATION

NOUN A **generator** is a machine for converting mechanical energy into electrical energy.

○ A hydroelectric plant is a plant in which the turbine generators are driven by falling water.

○ The hydraulic motors drive electrical generators to produce electricity.

ge|o|ther|mal pow|er /dziouθɜrmᵊl pauər/

ELECTRICAL POWER: GENERATION

NOUN **Geothermal power** is power that is generated using steam produced by heat coming from the melting center of the earth.

○ Conventional geothermal power stations involve surface pipelines bringing steam from widely distributed bore holes to central power stations.

○ Geothermal power plants have no smoky emission, but instead they emit water vapor.

OTHER TYPES OF POWER INCLUDE:

nuclear power, solar power, tidal power, wave power, wind power

---

gi|ga|hertz (ABBR **GHz**) /gɪgəhɜrts/ (gigahertz)

GENERAL

NOUN A **gigahertz** is a measure of frequency equivalent to one billion hertz or cycles per second.

○ In the early 21st century, 2.4 gigahertz transmissions have become increasingly utilized in high-end control of model vehicles and aircraft.

○ The term Radio Frequency means an electromagnetic signal at frequencies in the range extending from below 3 kilohertz to 300 gigahertz, which includes radio and television transmission.

G|P|S /dʒi pi ɛs/ (short for **Global Positioning System**)

INSTRUMENTATION, MEASURING, AND TESTING: DEVICES

ABBREVIATION **GPS** is a satellite-based navigation system in which two or more signals, received from satellites, are used to determine the receiver's position on the globe.

○ *The system uses GPS and an advanced timing system to provide flight tracking data on aircraft.*

○ *Land surveying, and navigation via land, water, and air use GPS to determine routes and locations based on radio waves from satellites.*

PRONUNCIATION

Three-letter abbreviations are usually pronounced as separate letters with the stress on the last syllable.

CHP /si eɪtʃ p̲i̲/
CPU /si pi y̲u̲/
DMM /di ɛm ɛ̲m̲/
RFI /ɑr ɛf a̲ɪ̲/
RMS /ɑr ɛm ɛ̲s̲/

---

gram (ABBR **g**, **gm**) /græ̲m/ (**grams**)

<u>GENERAL</u>

NOUN A **gram** is a unit of weight that is a one thousandth part of a kilogram.

○ *A weight of 5 grams is used as the controlling weight in a gravity-controlled instrument.*

○ *The metric system unit of heat is called a calorie, which is the energy needed to raise the temperature of 1 gram of water 1 degree Celsius.*

---

grid /grɪ̲d/ (**grids**)

<u>ELECTRICAL POWER: DISTRIBUTION</u>

NOUN The **grid** is the national network of transmission lines, pipes, and equipment through which electricity is distributed.

○ *Should the wind system produce less power, the breaker box shuts and opens power from the grid to be used.*

○ *Power systems are designed to meet customers' needs for harsh, remote environments where access to the electrical grid is not possible.*

---

ground[1] (In BRIT use **earth**) /gra̲ʊ̲nd/

<u>SEMICONDUCTOR AND ELECTRONIC CIRCUITRY</u>

NOUN The **ground** in an electric plug or piece of electrical equipment is the wire through which electricity passes into the earth, and makes the equipment safe.

○ *For safety, a ground wire is often connected between the individual electrical appliances in the house and the main electric switchboard or fusebox.*

○ *Regardless of the source of the disturbance, any voltage greater than 1V between neutral and ground generally will cause equipment malfunction.*

---

ground² (In Brit use **earth**) /graʊnd/ (**grounds, grounded, grounding**)

SEMICONDUCTOR AND ELECTRONIC CIRCUITRY

VERB If you **ground** an electrical circuit or device, you connect it to ground, to make it safe.

○ *We ground the outer case as an essential part of the safety system.*

○ *Grounding a fuse or breaker is an essential part of the safety system.*

---

ground|ed neu|tral /graʊndɪd nutrəl/

ELECTRICAL POWER

NOUN **Grounded neutral** is the situation in which the neutral wire of an electrical supply system is connected to ground.

○ *A grounded neutral fault cannot coexist with load current because this would result in large amounts of load current returning through ground, causing a ground fault to be detected.*

○ *Even with a grounded neutral the neutral wire carries power in normal operation, whereas the ground never carries power unless there is a fault.*

---

ground|ing (In Brit use **earthing**) /graʊndɪŋ/

CIRCUITS / ELECTRICAL POWER

NOUN **Grounding** is the act of connecting a conductor, or exposed conductive parts of an installation, to the earth.

○ *The grounding protects personnel from stray currents that could leak to the metallic enclosures.*

○ *A lightning rod and its associated grounding conductors provide protection because they divert the current from nonconducting parts of the structure.*

ground leak|age (In BRIT use **earth leakage**) /gra͟ʊnd li͟kɪdʒ/

ELECTRICAL POWER

NOUN **Ground leakage** is the flow of current from a live conductor to the earth through the insulation.

○ Electrical power systems must include devices to detect ground leakage currents of even small magnitude, and to disconnect power from the load circuit involved when such leakage currents are detected.

○ A ground fault detector protects an electrical power system against ground leakage currents.

ground leak|age cir|cuit break|er (In BRIT use **earth leakage circuit breaker**) /gra͟ʊnd li͟kɪdʒ sɜ͟ːrkɪt bre͟ɪkər/ (**ground leakage circuit breakers**)

ELECTRICAL POWER: POWER CONSUMPTION

NOUN A **ground leakage circuit breaker** is a protective device designed to protect both equipment and users from fault currents between the live and ground conductors.

○ The ground leakage circuit breaker turns the electricity supply off when current travels into the ground wire.

○ In some situations it is not possible to obtain an efficient grounding, so the supply authority will insist on the installation of a ground leakage circuit breaker.

ground re|turn (In BRIT use **earth return**) /gra͟ʊnd rɪtɜ͟ːrn/

SEMICONDUCTOR AND ELECTRONIC CIRCUITRY

NOUN **Ground return** is the return path for an electrical circuit made by connections to ground at each end.

○ Ground return involves using the ground as a return conductor, which allows a single wire to be used to carry current between two points.

○ Ground return is not as effective in dry ground as in damp ground.

Hh

half wave rec|ti|fi|er /hæf weɪv rɛktɪfaɪər/ (**half wave rectifiers**)

SEMICONDUCTOR AND ELECTRONIC CIRCUITRY

NOUN A **half wave rectifier** removes the negative component of an alternating signal leaving only the positive part.

○ A half wave rectifier will only give one peak per cycle, and for this and other reasons is only used in very small power supplies.

○ For a given effective DC output a half wave rectifier requires about twice the peak AC input voltage as does the full wave rectifier.

har|mon|ic dis|tor|tion (ABBR **HD**) /harmɒnɪk dɪstɔrʃᵊn/

COMMUNICATION: ANALOG

NOUN **Harmonic distortion** is the presence of frequencies in the output of a device that are not present in the input signal.

○ The inverter bridge must be followed by a filter to take out harmonic distortion and allow a controllable power flow.

○ Reducing the harmonic distortion of a system can be accomplished with centralized or localized harmonic filters.

H|D|T|V /eɪtʃ di ti vi/ (short for **high-definition television**)

COMMUNICATION

ABBREVIATION **HDTV** is an all-digital system for transmitting a TV signal with far greater resolution than the analog system.

○ HDTV brings an unprecedented level of detail and color to your TV viewing experience.

○ HDTV has 10 times more picture detail than analog signals.

heat sink /hɪt sɪŋk/ (**heat sinks**)

SEMICONDUCTOR AND ELECTRONIC CIRCUITRY

NOUN A **heat sink** is a metal plate that is specially designed to conduct and radiate heat away from an electrical component.

○ *The metal heat sink ensures good heat dispersal and allows a low hot-spot temperature.*

○ *Aluminum-cased wirewound resistors are designed to be attached to a heat sink to dissipate the heat.*

hen|ry (ABBR **H**) /hɛnri/ (**henries**)

CIRCUITS / ELECTRICAL POWER / COMPUTING AND CONTROL

NOUN A **henry** is a unit of electric inductance that is equal to 1 volt in a closed circuit when the electric current in the circuit varies uniformly at the rate of 1 ampere per second.

○ *An inductor's ability to store magnetic energy is measured by its inductance, in units of henries.*

○ *One henry of inductance exists when one volt of electromotive force is induced when the current is changing at the rate of one ampere per second.*

> **WORD ORIGINS**
>
> This word is named for **Joseph Henry** (1797–1878), the American physicist who discovered several important principles of electromagnetism.

hertz (ABBR **Hz**) /hɜrts/ (**hertz**)

GENERAL

NOUN A **hertz** is a measure of frequency, equal to one cycle per second.

○ *Your wall outlet gives 60 hertz of alternating current electricity in the USA.*

○ *Computer processors are commonly referred to by the speed that the CPU can process computer instructions per second measured in hertz and are one of the primary selling points of a computer.*

high fre|quen|cy (ABBR **HF**) /haɪ frɪkwənsi/

COMMUNICATION

NOUN **High frequency** is any radio frequency in the range of 3 to 30 MHz.

○ *Clocks, lasers, and other systems that need either strong resonance or high frequency stability need high-quality factors.*

○ *Humans find mid and high frequency noise to be the most annoying, because human ears are better equipped to hear these than low frequencies.*

high-pass fil|ter /haɪ pæs fɪltər/ (**high-pass filters**)

COMPUTING AND CONTROL

NOUN A **high-pass filter** is a filter designed to pass all frequencies above its cut-off frequency.

○ *A high-pass filter is used in an audio system to allow high frequencies to get through while filtering or cutting low frequencies.*

○ *In a serial digital data communication system, low-frequency signal components are often lost when the signal passes through a high-pass filter, such as an AC-coupling network.*

high-ten|sion (ABBR **HT**) /haɪ tɛnʃən/

ELECTRICAL POWER: DISTRIBUTION

ADJECTIVE A **high-tension** cable carries more than 1000 Volts between conductors and 600 Volts between conductors and ground.

○ *You need very high voltage for transmission on high-tension power lines.*

○ *There exists a need for an insulator device for use on high-tension AC power lines that prevents the accumulation of particulate contaminants to reduce the likelihood of a flashover event.*

high volt|age (ABBR **HV**) /haɪ voʊltɪdʒ/ (**high voltages**)

ELECTRICAL POWER: DISTRIBUTION

NOUN A **high voltage** system carries more than 1000 Volts between conductors and 600 Volts between conductors and ground.

○ *By using transformers, the voltage of the power can be stepped up to a high voltage so that the power may be distributed over long distances at low currents and hence low losses.*

○ The transformer allows a high voltage power supply to operate from a lower voltage source.

hy|dro|e|lec|tric /ˌhaɪdroʊɪˈlɛktrɪk/

ELECTRICAL POWER: GENERATION

ADJECTIVE A **hydroelectric** system generates electricity by water pressure.

○ A hydroelectric plant is a plant in which the turbine generators are driven by falling water.

○ A cam-shaped buoy rolls with the passing of waves, and the rolling action drives hydraulics, which run a hydroelectric generator.

hys|te|re|sis /hɪstəˈriːsɪs/

CIRCUITS / ELECTRICAL POWER

NOUN **Hysteresis** is something that happens with magnetic materials so that, if a varying magnetizing signal is applied, the resulting magnetism that is created follows the applied signal, but with a delay.

○ Hysteresis means that the magnitude of a resulting quantity is different during increases in the magnitude of the cause than during decreases, due to internal friction in a substance.

○ As a general term, hysteresis means a lag between input and output in a system upon a change in direction.

Ii

im|ag|i|nar|y op|er|a|tor /ɪmædʒɪnɛri ɒpəreɪtər/
(**imaginary operators**)

CIRCUITS / COMMUNICATION

NOUN An **imaginary operator** is the part of a complex number that defines the magnitude of the part of the complex number at right angles to the real number part. The symbol j is used for the imaginary operator.

○ If both the real and imaginary operators have a magnitude of 0.707 the amplitude will be 1 and the phase angle 45 degrees.

○ The imaginary operator simply is an anticlockwise rotation of 90 degrees.

▶ SYNONYM:
j operator

---

im|ped|ance /ɪmpiːdᵊns/

CIRCUITS / ELECTRICAL POWER / COMPUTING AND CONTROL

NOUN **Impedance** is a measure of the opposition to electrical flow, that is measured in ohms. The symbol Z is used for impedance.

○ If you are running two 16 ohm speaker cabinets in parallel, you must set or use an amplifier and attenuator with an impedance value of 8 ohms.

○ The primary winding is designed to have very low impedance, and hence has negligible effect on the main current.

---

im|pulse /ɪmpʌls/ (**impulses**)

CIRCUITS / ELECTRICAL POWER / COMPUTING AND CONTROL

NOUN An **impulse** is a disturbance of the voltage waveform that is less than about one millisecond.

○ The motor impulse is sufficient to accelerate the round to 750 meters per second in 2.3 seconds.

○ *When the system is subject to an impulse (or any signal of finite duration) it will respond with an output waveform which lasts past the duration of the input.*

---

in|duct|ance /ɪndʌktəns/

CIRCUITS / ELECTRICAL POWER / COMPUTING AND CONTROL

NOUN Inductance is the property of a circuit or coil that causes an electromotive force to be set up due to a rate of change of current in the circuit or coil. The symbol for inductance is L.

○ *The effects of capacitance and inductance are generally most significant at high frequencies.*

○ *For audio applications, inductors typically carry values of a few henries, while higher-frequency applications usually require much lower inductances in the milli- or microhenry ranges.*

---

in|duc|tion coil /ɪndʌkʃ°n kɔɪl/ (**induction coils**)

ELECTRICAL POWER

NOUN An **induction coil** is a transformer for producing a high voltage from a low voltage.

○ *A current flows through the induction coil to generate a high-frequency electromagnetic field.*

○ *An induction coil is an electrical device in common use as the ignition system or spark coil of internal-combustion engines.*

---

in|duc|tion heat|ing /ɪndʌkʃ°n hitɪŋ/

ELECTRICAL POWER

NOUN Induction heating is the heating of a conducting material as a result of the electric currents induced in it by an externally applied alternating magnetic field.

○ *Induction heating is used in heating metals and other conductive materials.*

○ *Whereas induction heating uses a varying magnetic field, dielectric heating employs a varying electric field.*

in|duc|tion mo|tor /ɪndʌkʃⁿn moʊtər/ (**induction motors**)

ELECTRICAL POWER: MOTOR OR GENERATOR

NOUN An **induction motor** is a type of brushless electric motor in which an alternating supply fed to the windings of the stator creates a magnetic field that induces a current in the windings of the rotor.

○ *An induction motor is an asynchronous AC motor where power is transferred to the rotor by electromagnetic induction, much like transformer action.*

○ *Since the induction motor has no DC field winding, there is no sustained field current in the rotor to provide flux as is the case with a synchronous machine.*

in|duc|tor /ɪndʌktər/ (**inductors**)

CIRCUITS / ELECTRICAL POWER / COMPUTING AND CONTROL

NOUN An **inductor** is a circuit element that is a wire wound into a coil to create a magnetic field.

○ *An inductor resists change in the flow of electric current through it, because it generates a magnetic field that acts to oppose the flow of current through it.*

○ *When two inductors are connected in series then their total inductance equals the sum of individual inductances.*

in|put/out|put (ABBR I/O) /ɪnpʊt aʊtpʊt/ (**input/outputs**)

COMPUTING AND CONTROL

NOUN The **input/output** of an electrical system or an information processing system such as a computer is the communication that comes into it from the outside world or travels from it to the outside world.

○ *The input/output quantities are shown on the rating plate of the machine.*

○ *One simple transformer specification is the input/output rating.*

in|stal|la|tion /ɪnstəleɪʃⁿn/ (**installations**)

ELECTRICAL POWER

NOUN An electrical **installation** is a combination of electrical equipment installed from a common electrical supply to fulfill a particular purpose.

○ *Induction generators are often used in wind turbines and some micro hydro installations due to their ability to produce useful power at varying rotor speeds.*

○ *All single-phase loads in an electrical installation with a three-phase supply should be evenly and reasonably distributed among the phases.*

in|su|la|tion /ɪnsəleɪʃⁿn/

CIRCUITS / ELECTRICAL POWER

NOUN **Insulation** is suitable non-conductive material enclosing, surrounding, or supporting a conductor.

○ *In the early days of cable-making, there would be current leaking through the insulation as well, but in modern cables, such leakage is negligible.*

○ *Insulation is non-conductive material used to prevent leakage of electric current from a conductor.*

in|su|la|tor /ɪnsəleɪtər/ (**insulators**)

CIRCUITS / ELECTRICAL POWER

NOUN An **insulator** is a non-conductor of electricity or heat.

○ *An insulator is a material of such low electrical conductivity that the flow of current through it can usually be neglected.*

○ *A material that permits the free passage of current is called a conductor and one that opposes the passage of current is called an insulator.*

in|te|grat|ed cir|cuit (ABBR **IC**) /ɪntɪɡreɪtɪd sɜrkɪt/ (**integrated circuits**)

SEMICONDUCTOR AND ELECTRONIC CIRCUITRY

NOUN An **integrated circuit** is a device that contains its own transistors, resistors, and diodes within itself.

○ *Today's radios are amazing pieces of modern technology, filled with low-power, high-performance, integrated circuits crammed into the smallest spaces.*

○ *A chip is also called an integrated circuit, which can contain millions of transistors.*

i|so|la|tion /aɪsəleɪʃⁿn/

CIRCUITS / ELECTRICAL POWER

NOUN **Isolation** is the degree to which a device can separate the electrical environment of its input from its output, while allowing the desired transmission to pass across the separation.

○ *Transformers are comprised of two or more magnetically coupled inductors and are appropriate when electrical isolation is required between input and output circuits of a switch-mode power supply.*

○ *The primary disadvantage of an autotransformer is that there is a direct physical connection between its primary and secondary circuits, so the electrical isolation of two sides is lost.*

i|so|la|tion trans|form|er /aɪsəleɪʃᵊn trænsfɔrmər/
(isolation transformers)

CIRCUITS / ELECTRICAL POWER

NOUN An **isolation transformer** is a transformer with physically separate primary and secondary windings, that prevent it from transferring unwanted noise from the input circuit to the output windings.

○ *An isolation transformer has separate windings and does not allow current to pass into the vessel from the utility connection.*

○ *The isolation transformer will reduce any voltage spikes that originate on the supply side before they are transferred to the load side.*

i|so|la|tor /aɪsəleɪtər/ **(isolators)**

CIRCUITS / ELECTRICAL POWER

NOUN An **isolator** is a mechanical switching device that, in the open position, allows for isolation of the input and output of a device.

○ *An isolator differs from a switch in that it is intended to be opened when the circuit is not carrying current.*

○ *An isolator is a device used for isolating a circuit or equipment from a source of power.*

Jj

jack /dʒæk/ (jacks)

NOUN A **jack** is a female socket with two or more terminals designed to receive a male plug that either makes or breaks the circuit.

○ *This type of product requires the user to plug and unplug the speaker cable into these individual jacks.*

○ *The signal from the output jack is typically fed into a power amplifier or sound system mixing board.*

joule (ABBR J) /dʒuːl/ (joules)

NOUN A **joule** is a measurement of energy or work, that, in mechanical systems, is equal to the force of one newton, moving an object a distance of one meter.

○ *Cellphones can have a maximum power output of 2W, which is 2 joules per second.*

○ *Average power is calculated by dividing joules by seconds over a period of one or more whole waveform cycles.*

WORD ORIGINS

This word is named for the English physicist **James Prescott Joule** (1818–1889) who established the theory behind the first law of thermodynamics.

junc|tion box /dʒʌŋkʃən bɒks/ (**junction boxes**)

GENERAL

NOUN A **junction box** is a box in which conductors or wires are split or terminated.

○ Where a three-phase circuit is used for single-phase loads a junction box is provided at each piece of equipment and single-phase supply is tapped.

○ A junction box is an enclosed distribution panel for the connection or branching of one or more electrical circuits.

J

Kar|naugh map (ABBR **K map**) /kɑrnɔ mæp/ (**Karnaugh maps**)

NOUN A **Karnaugh map** is a pictorial method used to minimize Boolean expressions without having to use Boolean algebra theorems. The Karnaugh map is named for US physicist Maurice Karnaugh (b. 1934).

- ○ *The Karnaugh map reduces the need for extensive calculations by taking advantage of humans' pattern-recognition capability.*
- ○ *Karnaugh maps are useful for detecting and eliminating race hazards, which can give rise to errors in digital logic.*

kil|o|gram (ABBR **kg**) /kɪləgræm/ (**kilograms**)

GENERAL

NOUN The **kilogram** is a metric unit of weight, equal to a thousand grams.

- ○ *Conventional capacitors provide less than 360 joules per kilogram of energy density.*
- ○ *The units of kilograms and newtons are often confused by non-engineers.*

kil|o|watt-hour (ABBR **kWh**) /kɪləwɑt ɑʊər/ (**kilowatt-hours**)

ELECTRICAL POWER: POWER CONSUMPTION

NOUN A **kilowatt-hour** is the standard unit of electricity supplied to the consumer, which is equal to 1 kilowatt acting for 1 hour.

- ○ *A 100-watt lamp operated for 10 hours consumes one kilowatt-hour of electricity.*
- ○ *If you wish to measure the energy consumed by certain equipment or certain circuits, a kilowatt-hour meter can be used.*

Ll

---

lag /læg/

ELECTRICAL POWER: MOTOR OR GENERATOR

NOUN **Lag** is the delay between voltage signal and the corresponding current signal.

- ○ *Motors generally cause a situation where there is a lag between the current and the voltage.*
- ○ *Server connections are often made up of many nodes, and the more nodes between you and the other person, the higher the possibility is of lags occurring.*

---

lag|ging load /lægɪŋ loʊd/ (lagging loads)

ELECTRICAL POWER: POWER CONSUMPTION

NOUN A **lagging load** is one where the phase of the current lags behind the phase of the voltage when supplied with an alternating voltage.

- ○ *Connecting capacitors near the point of the lagging load cancels the lagging current and allows for most efficient use of conductors and other equipment.*
- ○ *A lagging load is a reactive load in which inductive reactance exceeds the capacitive reactance and therefore carries a lagging current with respect to the voltage across its terminals.*

---

lam|i|na|tion /læmɪneɪʃᵊn/ (laminations)

ELECTRICAL POWER: TRANSFORMERS

NOUN A **lamination** is one of a set of iron plates forming the core of an electrical transformer.

- ○ *The armature of an AC generator is the assembly of windings and metal core laminations in which the output voltage is induced.*
- ○ *Higher quality transformers use thinner laminations and better materials to get higher efficiency.*

La|place trans|form /ləplɑs trænsfɔrm/ (**Laplace transforms**)

COMMUNICATION: ANALOG

NOUN The **Laplace transform** is a powerful tool formulated to solve a wide variety of initial-value problems. The Laplace transform is named for French mathematician Pierre-Simon Laplace (1749–1827).

○ *Like the Fourier transform, the Laplace transform is used for solving differential and integral equations.*

○ *Laplace transform turns integral equations and differential equations to polynomial equations, which are much easier to solve.*

large-scale in|te|gra|tion (ABBR **LSI**) /lɑrdʒ skeɪl ɪntɪɡreɪʃən/

SEMICONDUCTOR AND ELECTRONIC CIRCUITRY

NOUN **Large-scale integration** is a situation in which a chip has tens of thousands of transistors on it.

○ *A microprocessor is a clock-driven semiconductor device consisting of electronic logic circuits manufactured by using a large-scale integration technique.*

○ *Large-scale integration technology was used to place thousands of discrete solid-state components on a single IC chip.*

lead /liːd/ (**leads, led, leading**)

ELECTRICAL POWER: MOTOR OR GENERATOR

VERB If a voltage signal **leads** the corresponding current signal, then it is in advance of it.

○ *When the phase of the voltage is ahead in time of the phase of the current, then the voltage is said to lead the current.*

○ *If the current is a cosine and the voltage is a sine then the current leads the voltage by ninety degrees.*

leak|age cur|rent /liːkɪdʒ kɜrənt/

ELECTRICAL POWER

NOUN A **leakage current** is an electric current in an unwanted conductive path under normal operating conditions.

- If the conductors are separated by a material with a small conductivity rather than a perfect dielectric, then a small leakage current flows directly between them.
- A small leakage current flows through the sensor even when the output is off.

L|E|D /ɛl i diː/ (short for **light-emitting diode**)

ELECTRONICS COMPONENTS

ABBREVIATION An **LED** is a semiconductor device that emits light.

- LED lights are much more efficient, working with only a fraction of the energy needed even by fluorescent lights even though offering much higher luminescence.
- A 3 digit LED display shows the output voltage of each individual channel.

light|ning rod /ˈlaɪtnɪŋ rɒd/ (**lightning rods**)

ELECTRICAL POWER

NOUN A **lightning rod** is a grounded metallic rod set up on a structure like a building to protect it from lightning.

- A lightning rod and its associated grounding conductors provide protection because they divert the current from nonconducting parts of the structure.
- To avoid accidents, the quality of the electrical connection between ground and the lightning rod is checked from time to time.

line /laɪn/ (**lines**)

CIRCUITS / ELECTRICAL POWER / COMPUTING AND CONTROL

NOUN A **line** is a conducting wire, cable, or circuit for making connections between pieces of electrical apparatus, such as a cable for electric power transmission or telecommunications.

- When a fuse is blown, the electricity is blocked from continuing down the line, but the supply voltage is still present.
- Many wind turbines are not fitted with output power control systems that are capable of stable line voltage regulation.

liq|uid-crys|tal dis|play (ABBR **LCD**) /ˈlɪkwɪd krɪstəl dɪspleɪ/ (**liquid-crystal displays**)

INSTRUMENTATION, MEASURING, AND TESTING

NOUN A **liquid-crystal display** is a flat panel display, electronic visual display, or video display that uses the light modulating properties of liquid crystals.

○ *A liquid-crystal display device is visible in all light conditions, can display changes instantly, and consumes less power than other display devices.*

○ *Liquid-crystal display produces no illumination of its own, but depends entirely on illumination falling on it from an external source for its visual effect.*

> **RELATED WORDS**
>
> Compare **liquid-crystal display** with **cathode ray tube** in which a vacuum tube containing an electron gun and a fluorescent screen is used to display images.

lith|i|um bat|ter|y (ABBR Li) /lɪθiəm bætəri/ (lithium batteries)

GENERAL

NOUN A **lithium battery** is a type of battery used for low-power, high-reliability, long-life applications, such as clocks, cameras and calculators.

○ *Lithium batteries can easily support the brief, heavy current demands of devices such as digital cameras, and they maintain a higher voltage for a longer period than alkaline cells.*

○ *Over 95 percent of the heart pacemakers use a lithium battery to power the pacing systems, and it has a 7 to 10 year life in these applications.*

live /laɪv/

CIRCUITS / ELECTRICAL POWER

ADJECTIVE A **live** electrical circuit is connected to a source of electric power.

○ *Safety means that there are no grounded places which can be accidentally touched while also touching any part of a live circuit.*

○ *If you do not disconnect the phase line, the entire circuit is live and cannot be safely handled for maintenance.*

live wire /laɪv waɪər/ (live wires)

CIRCUITS / ELECTRICAL POWER

NOUN A **live wire** is a wire carrying an electric current.

○ *If something goes wrong inside and the live wire gets accidentally connected to some metal part, the circuit breaker will blow, protecting the user from an unpleasant sensation or even electrocution.*

○ *To transmit power with single-phase alternating current, we need two wires – live wire and neutral.*

load¹ /loʊd/ (loads)

ELECTRICAL POWER: POWER CONSUMPTION

NOUN The **load** of a machine, generator, or circuit is the power that it delivers.

○ *Different houses in the street are placed on different phases of the supply so that the load is balanced, or spread evenly, across the three phases when a lot of consumers are connected.*

○ *The aircraft generator is supplying a load of 90kW at a power factor of 0.75 lagging.*

load² /loʊd/ (loads, loaded, loading)

ELECTRICAL POWER: POWER CONSUMPTION

VERB If you **load** an electrical device, such as a generator, you draw power from it.

○ *During continuous operations, the motor can be loaded up to the rated torque.*

○ *If the series wound motor is not loaded, the rotation speed can rise up to inadmissible high values and can destroy the motor mechanically.*

load³ /loʊd/ (loads)

CIRCUITS / ELECTRICAL POWER / COMPUTING AND CONTROL

NOUN A **load** is a device that receives or dissipates the power from an amplifier, oscillator, generator, or some other source of signals.

○ *All power drawn by the load passes via the inverter.*

○ *An operating source is a source of electrical power that is delivering power to a load.*

load fac|tor /loʊd fæktər/ (**load factors**)

ELECTRICAL POWER: POWER CONSUMPTION

NOUN A **load factor** is the ratio of the average electric load to the peak load over a period of time.

○ The load factor is the actual kilowatt-hours delivered on a system in a given period of time, as opposed to the total possible kilowatt-hours that could be delivered in a given period of time.

○ The assumption of load factor in the electrical system can have a significant effect on the total number of conduits and conductors that are required in the distribution system.

load|ing coil /loʊdɪŋ kɔɪl/ (**loading coils**)

COMMUNICATION

NOUN A **loading coil** is an inductance coil inserted at regular intervals and in series with the conductors of a transmission line in order to improve its function.

○ A loading coil is a coil that does not provide coupling to any other circuit, but is inserted in a circuit to increase its inductance.

○ In a loading coil with very small distributed capacitance to the outside world compared to termination impedance, current has to be equal.

loss /lɔs/

ELECTRICAL POWER: POWER CONSUMPTION

NOUN **Loss** in an electrical system is a measure of the power lost, which is expressed as the ratio of or difference between the input power and the output power.

○ Transmitting energy at high voltages minimizes the loss due to conductor resistance.

○ While power can be dissipated in other resistors, there is no power loss in the battery because there is no resistance.

loss|es /lɔsɪz/

CIRCUITS / ELECTRICAL POWER / COMPUTING AND CONTROL

NOUN **Losses** are energy and capacity lost in the operation of an electric system.

○ *By using transformers, the voltage of the power can be stepped up to a high voltage so that the power may be distributed over long distances at low currents and hence low losses.*

○ *Losses occur principally as energy transformations from kilowatt hours to waste heat in electrical conductors and apparatus.*

---

low-ten|sion (ABBR **LT**) /loʊ tɛnʃᵊn/

ELECTRICAL POWER

ADJECTIVE **Low-tension** equipment carries, is subjected to, or is capable of operating at a low voltage.

○ *The windings with the lower number of turns are called the low-tension windings.*

○ *The ordinary induction or spark coil may be called an intermittent current transformer, since it transforms an intermittent low-tension primary current into an intermittent high-tension current.*

L|S|B /ɛl ɛs bi/

COMPUTING AND CONTROL: DIGITAL

ABBREVIATION In a binary number, the **LSB** is the least weighted bit in the number.

○ *Most serial communications designs send the data bits within each byte LSB first.*

○ *The accuracy and linearity values of a converter are specified in the data sheet in units of the LSB of the code.*

Mm

---

mag|net|ic flux /mægnɛtɪk flʌks/

CIRCUITS / ELECTRICAL POWER

NOUN **Magnetic flux** is a measure of quantity of magnetism.

- ○ The magnetic flux created by the field windings follows the path of least magnetic reluctance.
- ○ A magnetic circuit is made up of one or more closed loop paths containing a magnetic flux.

---

mag|ne|to|mo|tive force /mægnɪtoʊmoʊtɪv fɔrs/

ELECTRICAL POWER

NOUN **Magnetomotive force** is the force that sets up a magnetic field within and around an object.

- ○ The duration of each positive and negative voltage is controlled so as to provide alternating positive and negative peaks of current excitation or magnetomotive force of uniformly equal amplitudes.
- ○ The unit of magnetomotive force is the ampere-turn, represented by a steady, direct electric current of one ampere flowing in a single-turn loop of electrically conducting material in a vacuum.

---

meg|a|bits /mɛgəbɪts/

GENERAL

NOUN **Megabits** are one million bits per second.

- ○ At current broadband rates of 6 megabits a second, a high-definition movie downloads in 90 minutes.
- ○ Most Internet providers offer speeds up to 7 megabits or 30 megabits per second.

> **WORD BUILDER**
> **mega-** = one million
>
> The prefix **mega-** appears in several words meaning "million:"
> **megahertz, megavolt, megawatt.**

---

meg|a|hertz (ABBR **MHz**) /mɛgəhɜrts/ (**megahertz**)
CIRCUITS / COMMUNICATION

NOUN A **megahertz** is a measurement of frequency equal to a million cycles per second.

○ The megahertz is a unit of alternating current or electromagnetic wave frequency equal to one million hertz.

○ The VHF radio band spans from 30 to 328.6 megahertz.

---

meg|a|volt (ABBR **MV**) /mɛgəvoʊlt/ (**megavolts**)
CIRCUITS / ELECTRICAL POWER

NOUN A **megavolt** is one million volts.

○ An average bolt of negative lightning carries a current of 30 kiloamperes, transfers a charge of 5 coulombs, has a potential difference of about 100 megavolts, and dissipates 500 megajoules.

○ The layer of insulating aluminum oxide on the surface of the aluminum plate can withstand an electric field strength of the order of 25 megavolts per meter.

---

meg|a|watt /mɛgəwɒt/ (**megawatts**)
CIRCUITS / ELECTRICAL POWER

NOUN A **megawatt** is one million watts.

○ This 180- to 190-mile line, projected to carry 1,200 megawatts, will carry electricity to approximately one million homes.

○ It would take 1,500 wind turbines spread over 20 square kilometers to produce the same electricity as a 1,000 megawatt nuclear power station.

---

me|ter (ABBR **m**) /mitər/ (**meters**)
INSTRUMENTATION, MEASURING, AND TESTING: INSTRUMENT

NOUN A **meter** is a metric unit of length equal to 100 centimeters.

○ Though the standard covers only transmissions over distances up to 15 meters, it is often possible to ensure correct transmission over greater distances using high-quality shielded cable.

○ To power a modern home on a good site, the blades of a wind turbine would need to span about 5 meters from tip to tip.

---

mi|cro|amp /maɪkroʊæmp/ (**microamps**) (short for **microampere**)

CIRCUITS / COMMUNICATION

NOUN A **microamp** is a millionth part of an amp.

○ Because of very low duty cycles, average currents are therefore in the microamp range enabling button cell battery power sources to last up to a year.

○ A change of even several hundred volts across the gate usually causes at most a small fraction of a microamp to flow.

---

mi|cro|phone /maɪkrəfoʊn/ (**microphones**)

COMMUNICATION

NOUN A **microphone** is an electromechanical transducer that converts sound pressure into an electrical signal.

○ Our wireless microphone systems deliver a true reproduction of your voice.

○ Since the microphone built into the data recorder is provided normally for recording, environmental sounds can always be recorded during measurement.

---

mi|cro|pro|ces|sor /maɪkroʊprɒsɛsər/ (**microprocessors**)

SEMICONDUCTOR AND ELECTRONIC CIRCUITRY: DIGITAL

NOUN A **microprocessor** is a large-scale integrated circuit that can be programmed to perform arithmetic and logic functions and to manipulate data.

○ A microprocessor is a small chip part to control functions of digital systems like music players, electronic calculators, computers, and others.

○ The microprocessor is a CPU circuit contained within a silicon chip.

mi|cro|switch /maɪkrəswɪtʃ/ (microswitches)

ELECTRONICS COMPONENTS

NOUN A **microswitch** is a switch that operates by small movements of a lever.

○ A microswitch for controlling auxiliary circuits may be fitted to either side of the contactor.

○ The microswitch activates the electrical current to heat the element.

mi|cro|wave /maɪkrouweɪv/ (microwaves)

COMMUNICATION

NOUN A **microwave** is a product of electromagnetic radiation with wavelengths ranging from very short radio waves to almost infra-red region.

○ A cellphone emits microwave energy, and technically this radiation could cook food if it was much, much stronger, and if it was focused.

○ Wireless cable sends multiple channels of video programming by microwave transmission from an antenna rather than by cable.

mil|li|amp (ABBR mA) /mɪliæmp/ (milliamps)

CIRCUITS / COMMUNICATION

NOUN A **milliamp** is a unit for measuring electrical current equal to one thousandth of an ampere.

○ To satisfy a 5 milliamp trip level, the signal processor must be designed to respond to a transformer primary excitation of 0.005 ampere-turns.

○ Traditionally, a differential current transformer is utilized to sense when the 5 milliamp threshold is exceeded.

m|k|s sys|tem /ɛm keɪ ɛs sɪstəm/ (mks systems)

GENERAL

NOUN The **mks system** is the metric system in which the meter, kilogram, and the second are the fundamental units.

○ The mks system is a system of units of measurement based on the metric system.

○ A pascal is a unit of pressure in the mks system equivalent to one newton per square meter.

mo|dem /ˈmoʊdəm/ (**modems**)

COMMUNICATION: ANALOG

NOUN A **modem** is a hardware device that converts digital computer data into analog tones that can be transmitted over dial-up telephone circuits.

○ Analog modems convert the digital (binary) signal from the computer into an analog signal that the old style telephone network understands.

○ A broadband modem may share the utility data communications channel for the purpose of Internet access and other computer type services.

mod|u|late /ˈmɒdʒəleɪt/ (**modulates, modulated, modulating**)

COMMUNICATION: ANALOG

VERB To **modulate** a current is to cause it to vary by a process of modulation.

○ In AM radio, the signal is used to modulate the amplitude of the carrier.

○ The voltage regulator operates by modulating the small field current in order to produce a constant voltage at the stator output.

mod|u|la|tion /ˈmɒdʒəleɪʃən/

COMMUNICATION: ANALOG

NOUN **Modulation** is the act or process of giving a wave or signal the amplitude or frequency of another wave or signal.

○ In telecommunications, modulation is the process of conveying a message signal, for example a digital bit stream or an analog audio signal, inside another signal that can be physically transmitted.

○ At the receiving end of the communication system, the depth of modulation of the received signal is compared with that of the test signal in each of a number of frequency bands.

mo|tor /ˈmoʊtər/ (**motors**)

ELECTRICAL POWER: MOTOR OR GENERATOR

NOUN A **motor** is a rotating device that converts electrical power into mechanical power.

○ *An electric motor supplies 5 kW of power when operating at an efficiency of 75 percent.*

○ *A single-phase motor consists of two stator windings, two capacitors, a centrifugal switch and a rotor.*

---

mo|tor gen|er|a|tor set /ˈmoʊtər dʒɛnəreɪtər sɛt/ (**motor generator sets**)

ELECTRICAL POWER: MOTOR OR GENERATOR

NOUN A **motor generator set** is an alternating current motor that is attached to a generator.

○ *The only true way to get a pure sine wave is to use a motor generator set where you use the DC power to run a DC motor which then runs an AC alternator producing true sinusoid wave forms.*

○ *Large cascade transformer units are supplied power through a separate motor generator set or by means of voltage regulators.*

---

mul|ti|me|ter /ˈmʌltɪmɪtər/ (**multimeters**)

INSTRUMENTATION, MEASURING, AND TESTING: INSTRUMENT

NOUN A **multimeter** is an electrical test instrument that measures several values, usually voltage, current, and resistance.

○ *The oscilloscope does not generally have very much accuracy for making measurements as compared with a multimeter, which will give more accurate measurements of direct current.*

○ *If you hook up two multimeters to measure current and voltage and then multiply the readings together, you get apparent power in volt amps.*

Nn

na|no|volt (ABBR nV) /ˈnænəvoʊlt/ (nanovolts)

CIRCUITS / COMMUNICATION

NOUN A **nanovolt**, which is equal to one billionth of a volt, is a unit used to measure the force of an electric current.

○ *When voltages are extremely small they may be expressed in nanovolts.*

○ *One millivolt equals a thousand nanovolts.*

neg|a|tive feed|back /ˈnɛgətɪv ˈfiːdbæk/

COMPUTING AND CONTROL

NOUN **Negative feedback** is a situation in which a signal that is proportional to the output signal but has a phase that opposes the input signal is fed back to the input of an amplifier, or other circuit.

○ *The negative feedback into the difference amplifier allows the amplifier to compare the input to the actual output.*

○ *At the transistor level, device noise can be sensed and reduced with negative feedback.*

> **RELATED WORDS**
>
> Compare **negative feedback** with **positive feedback**, which is feedback in which the returning signal improves the effect of the input signal.

net|work /ˈnɛtwɜːrk/ (networks)

ELECTRICAL POWER

NOUN A **network** is a system of transmission and distribution lines that are connected together and operated to allow multiple power supply to any of the main points on it.

○ *The presence of various voltage and power levels causes problems in finding out the currents or voltages at different points in the network.*

○ *Inrush current is the temporary current observed in a network when electrical devices are energized, generally due to the magnetic circuits of the devices.*

---

neu|tral /nutrəl/

ELECTRICAL POWER

NOUN **Neutral** is the point that is common to all phases of a polyphase circuit, a conductor to that point, or the return conductor in a single phase circuit.

○ *At the load end of the circuit the return legs of the three-phase circuits can be coupled together at the neutral point, where the three currents sum to zero.*

○ *The windings may be connected in one of several configurations and the neutrals of windings that are normally grounded in service are connected to ground.*

---

new|ton (ABBR **N**) /nutᵊn/ (**newtons**)

GENERAL

NOUN One **newton** is a unit of force equal to the force needed to move a one kilogram mass by one meter per second per second.

○ *The charge is given in coulombs, the velocity in meters per second, so that the force is in newtons.*

○ *The unit of force is the newton where one newton is one kilogram meter per second squared.*

> **WORD ORIGINS**
>
> This word is named for **Sir Isaac Newton** (1642–1727), the great English mathematician and physicist who discovered gravity.

---

nod|al a|nal|y|sis /noʊdᵊl ənælɪsɪs/

SEMICONDUCTOR AND ELECTRONIC CIRCUITRY: ANALOG

NOUN **Nodal analysis** is a method of analyzing circuits based on defining node voltages as the variables.

○ *The technique of nodal analysis can be used to analyze circuits with reactive components.*

○ *Solving circuits with a free floating voltage source using the nodal analysis technique can be a bit tricky at first.*

---

node /noʊd/ (**nodes**)

SEMICONDUCTOR AND ELECTRONIC CIRCUITRY

NOUN A **node** is a point of connection between two or more elements or branches in a network.

○ *Ground can be placed anywhere for convenience, but it is mostly placed on a node with the most connections.*

○ *Since there could be multiple branches carrying very different currents between any pair of nodes, we must explicitly identify the branch of the controlling current.*

---

noise /nɔɪz/

CIRCUITS / COMMUNICATION

NOUN **Noise** is an unwanted random signal in the form of a voltage or current in an electrical circuit that makes the information more difficult to identify.

○ *Capacitors are used to reduce signal noise, and to prevent electromechanical contacts from burning.*

○ *The surface conditions of the overhead conductors subjected to high voltage stresses and varying atmospheric condition greatly influence the magnitude of the noise voltage produced.*

NOR gate /nɔr geɪt/ (**NOR gates**)

ELECTRONICS COMPONENTS: DIGITAL

NOUN A **NOR gate** is a digital logic gate that gives an output of 0 when any of its inputs are 1, otherwise 1.

○ *NOR gates can be made to produce a variety of logic gates, including OR and AND gates.*

○ *The output of the NOR gate is a logic 0 as long as the input voltage is below the threshold.*

nor|mal|ly-closed /nɔrməli kloʊzd/

CIRCUITS / ELECTRICAL POWER / COMPUTING AND CONTROL

ADJECTIVE **Normally-closed** switch contacts are in a closed state at rest.

○ If the temperature of any of these heater elements reaches a critical point, a normally-closed switch contact will spring open.

○ The provision of a pilot valve in the assembly represents a simple means for converting a normally-closed valve into a normally-open valve with a minimum amount of modification.

nor|mal|ly-o|pen /nɔrməli oʊpən/

CIRCUITS / ELECTRICAL POWER / COMPUTING AND CONTROL

ADJECTIVE **Normally-open** switch contacts are in an open state at rest.

○ In many applications normally-open valves are required which close when the solenoid pilot is energized.

○ Contactors typically have multiple contacts, and those contacts are usually normally-open, so that power to the load is shut off when the coil is de-energized.

N

nu|cle|ar pow|er /nukliər paʊər/

ELECTRICAL POWER: GENERATION

NOUN **Nuclear power** is power released in nuclear reactions that can be converted to electric power.

○ Availability of cheap and reliable nuclear power may stifle use of other forms of power, particularly if it is perceived as less polluting.

○ In a nuclear power plant, energy is generated from the splitting of the nuclei of uranium atoms.

Oo

ohm /oʊm/ (ohms)

CIRCUITS / ELECTRICAL POWER / COMPUTING AND CONTROL

NOUN An **ohm** is a unit of measurement of electric resistance. The symbol for an ohm is Ω.

○ One ampere is the unit of measurement of electrical current produced in a circuit by 1 volt acting through a resistance of 1 ohm.

○ With an ordinary coil of around 10,000 ohms resistance, the most powerful arc would be produced with about 12,000 alternations per second.

Ohm's law /oʊmz lɔ/

CIRCUITS / ELECTRICAL POWER / COMPUTING AND CONTROL

NOUN **Ohm's law** is a law that states that the voltage across a resistor is directly proportional to the current flowing through the resistance. Ohm's law is named for German physicist Georg Ohm (1789–1854).

○ A simple formula, Ohm's law, is used to show the relationship of current, voltage, and resistance.

○ We can calculate, using Ohm's law, what resistor is needed to get a specific current.

op amp /ɒp æmp/ (op amps) (short for **operational amplifier**)

COMPUTING AND CONTROL

NOUN An **op amp** is a high gain amplifier to which feedback may be applied to control and tailor its operation.

○ Since the op amp is powered asymmetrically, the output is a half-wave rectified alternating voltage.

○ A current source can be designed in a variety of different ways, but one of the most basic requires just an inexpensive op amp and two resistors connected in a inverting configuration.

o|pen cir|cuit /ˈoʊpən sɜːrkɪt/ (**open circuits**)

CIRCUITS / ELECTRICAL POWER / COMPUTING AND CONTROL

NOUN An **open circuit** is a circuit element that has an impedance approaching zero.

○ If you were to use a voltage meter, you would find zero volts after an open circuit.

○ If the voltage is more than 60 percent of its open circuit voltage rating, the system will be affected by the capacitive current.

OR gate /ɔːr geɪt/ (**OR gates**)

ELECTRONICS COMPONENTS: DIGITAL

NOUN An **OR gate** is a digital logic gate that gives an output of 1 when any of its inputs are 1, otherwise 0.

○ An OR gate performs like two switches in parallel supplying a light, so that when either of the switches is closed the light is on.

○ A starting point generator is connected to one input of the OR gate and a digital processor unit is connected to the other input.

os|cil|lo|scope /ˈɒsɪləskoʊp/ (**oscilloscopes**)

INSTRUMENTATION, MEASURING, AND TESTING: INSTRUMENT

NOUN An **oscilloscope** is an instrument that displays voltage or current against a base of time.

○ An oscilloscope is helpful in determining if the amplitude of the input waveform needs to be increased.

○ An oscilloscope check showed that modulation was limited to about 80 percent.

out|age /ˈaʊtɪdʒ/ (**outages**)

ELECTRICAL POWER: DISTRIBUTION

NOUN **Outage** is the period during which a generating unit, transmission line, or other facility is out of service.

○ High energy resolution reduces energy loss due to power outage.

○ Some peak loads continue to grow, potentially overloading these transformers and inevitably leading to outages.

out|let /aʊtlɪt/ (**outlets**)

ELECTRICAL POWER: POWER CONSUMPTION

NOUN An electrical **outlet** is a point in a wiring system from which current can be taken to supply electrical devices.

○ If someone plugs in a coffeepot on the same outlet as your charger, they will trip the breaker.

○ The devices that you want to run are plugged into the outlets on the front of the inverter.

o|ver|cur|rent de|tec|tion /oʊvərkɜrənt dɪtɛkʃ°n/

ELECTRICAL POWER

NOUN **Overcurrent detection** is a method of establishing that the value of current in a circuit exceeds a particular value for a particular length of time.

○ Overcurrent detection must be able to sense and open the circuit when its rating is exceeded for a specified amount of time (such as 125 percent for 30 seconds or 300 percent for 5 seconds).

○ A time-compensated overcurrent detection circuit shuts off a DC motor during large overcurrent conditions caused by actual constraints on the motor.

o|ver|load /oʊvərloʊd/

ELECTRICAL POWER: POWER CONSUMPTION

NOUN **Overload** is a situation in which extra power is taken from an electrical supply, and the increased current causes the cables to heat up, which may end in an electrical fault.

○ In the case of overload, the corresponding switch on the breaker panel trips, cutting off only that part of the home or business.

○ This series provides protection of AC or DC loads against damage from overload currents.

Pp

par|al|lel res|o|nance /pærəlɛl rɛzənəns/

SEMICONDUCTOR AND ELECTRONIC CIRCUITRY: ANALOG

NOUN **Parallel resonance** is a resonance condition that usually occurs in parallel resonant circuits, where the voltage becomes a maximum for a given current.

○ *Being a parallel resonance means the impedance is high and inrush surge current relatively low compared to a simple capacitor.*

○ *Series resonance produces voltage amplification and parallel resonance causes current multiplication within an electrical system.*

par|i|ty bit /pæriti bɪt/ (**parity bits**)

COMPUTING AND CONTROL: DIGITAL

NOUN In binary notation, a **parity bit** is an additional bit that is attached to each code group so that the total number of 1s being transmitted is either odd or even.

○ *When parity is used with a serial port, an extra bit is sent with each data character, arranged so that the number of 1 bits in each character, including the parity bit, is always odd or always even.*

○ *For the PC to receive the nine bits, it is necessary to treat the ninth bit as a parity bit.*

pas|cal (ABBR **Pa**) /pæskæl/ (**pascals**)

GENERAL

NOUN A **pascal** is a unit of pressure, where one pascal is equal to the force of one newton exerted on one square meter.

○ *Because the human ear perceives pressure changes logarithmically over a large range, the sound pressure level is measured in pascals and converted to decibels.*

○ *The standard way to rate microphone sensitivity is to apply a 1 kHz sound source equal to one pascal and then measure the output level and express it in mV/PA.*

WORD ORIGINS

This word is named for **Blaise Pascal** (1623–62), the French mathematician and physicist.

---

peak /piːk/

CIRCUITS / ELECTRICAL POWER

ADJECTIVE The **peak** value is the maximum value of an alternating or other waveform.

○ *The peak current observed subsequent to the fault occurrence is essentially due to discharging of the inverter output capacitors.*

○ *Since an alternating voltage of 500 volts (rms) has a peak value of 707 volts, a capacitor to which it is applied should have a working voltage of at least 750 volts.*

peak load /piːk loʊd/ (**peak loads**)

ELECTRICAL POWER: POWER CONSUMPTION

NOUN A **peak load** is the maximum load on an electrical power-supply system.

○ *There may be a loss between station or substation and translating device of 15 percent during the 1 or 2 hours of the evening peak load in the winter months.*

○ *Unlike coal power stations, which can take more than 12 hours to start up from cold, the hydroelectric plant can be brought into service in a few minutes, ideal to meet a peak load demand.*

peak-to-peak val|ue /piːk tə piːk væljuː/ (**peak-to-peak values**)

CIRCUITS / ELECTRICAL POWER

NOUN **Peak-to-peak value** is the maximum voltage change occurring during one cycle of alternating voltage or current.

○ *The peak-to-peak value of an AC voltage is defined as the difference between its positive peak and its negative peak.*

○ *When determining the peak-to-peak value on the oscilloscope, one or two peaks that are considerably greater than the rest of the waveform should be ignored.*

pe|ri|od /pɪəriəd/ (**periods**)

CIRCUITS / ELECTRICAL POWER / COMPUTING AND CONTROL

NOUN A **period** is the duration between repetitions of a waveform cycle.

○ *Average power is calculated by dividing joules by seconds over a period of one or more whole waveform cycles.*

○ *When capturing waveforms with long periods, the total time needed to capture the waveform is dominated by the time it takes the waveform to make the requisite number of repetitions.*

pe|ri|od|ic func|tion /pɪərɪɒdɪk fʌŋkʃᵊn/ (**periodic functions**)

CIRCUITS / ELECTRICAL POWER / COMPUTING AND CONTROL

NOUN A **periodic function** is a function that repeats itself after a definite period.

○ *The period of a periodic function is the smallest time interval over which the function repeats itself.*

○ *A sinusoidal waveform is a periodic function, which means it continually repeats itself after a fixed time interval.*

per|me|a|bil|i|ty /pɜrmiəbɪlɪti/

CIRCUITS / ELECTRICAL POWER

NOUN **Permeability** is a measure of how easily magnetic lines of force can pass through a material.

○ *The permeability of a material is defined as the constant of proportionality between the magnetic flux density and the magnetic field.*

○ *It takes less current flow to achieve a given flux density if a material exhibits a high permeability.*

per|mit|tiv|i|ty /pɜrmɪtɪvɪti/

CIRCUITS / ELECTRICAL POWER / COMPUTING AND CONTROL

NOUN The **permittivity** of a material is a measure of how easily electric lines of force can pass through it.

○ Permittivity is analogous to magnetic permeability, and it specifies the ease with which electric flux is permitted to pass through a given dielectric material.

○ The permittivity of a material is the ratio of the electric flux density to the electric field strength in that material.

---

per u|nit (ABBR **pu**) /pər yunɪt/

ELECTRICAL POWER

PHRASE **Per unit** is a way of expressing the value of a quantity in terms of a reference or base quantity.

○ In a per unit system each system variable or quantity is normalized with respect to its own base value.

○ Calculations are simplified because quantities expressed as per unit are the same regardless of the voltage level.

---

phase /feɪz/ (**phases**)

GENERAL

NOUN A **phase** is one of the circuits in a system in which there are two or more alternating voltages displaced by equal amounts in phase.

○ In many situations only a single phase is needed to supply street lights or residential consumers.

○ Unbalanced three-phase circuits are indicated by abnormally high currents in one or more of the phases.

P

---

phase dif|fer|ence /feɪz dɪfərəns/ (**phase differences**)

CIRCUITS / ELECTRICAL POWER / COMPUTING AND CONTROL

NOUN **Phase difference** is the difference in phase angle between two sinusoids or phasors.

○ In a three-phase system, the phase difference between conductors is one-third of a cycle.

○ It is the capacitance from the coil to the outside world that controls current distribution in the inductor and produces phase difference in current at each end.

phas|or /ˈfeɪzər/ (phasors)

SEMICONDUCTOR AND ELECTRONIC CIRCUITRY: ANALOG

NOUN A **phasor** is a rotating vector representing a quantity, such as an alternating current or voltage, that varies sinusoidally.

○ A phasor representation is a simple way of reducing the complexities of handling single frequency circuits.

○ A phasor gives answers for both magnitude and phase which are necessary for alternating current circuit analysis.

pho|to|cell /ˈfoʊtoʊsɛl/ (photocells) (short for **photo-electric cell**)

ELECTRONICS COMPONENTS

NOUN A **photocell** is a device that is used to detect and measure light.

○ The dusk to dawn photocell sensor switch will switch items such as lights and fans on during the night and off during the day.

○ A photocell sensor can be regarded as a transducer that is used to detect the light intensity.

plant /plænt/

ELECTRICAL POWER

NOUN A **plant** is a place that contains electric generators and other equipment for producing electric energy.

○ Diesel or gas-fired engines are the principal types used in electric plants.

○ The utility is a commercial power source that supplies electrical power to specific facilities from a large central power plant.

plug /plʌg/ (plugs)

GENERAL

NOUN A **plug** is a small plastic device with two or three metal pins, that is intended to be attached to a flexible cable, and that fits into the holes of a socket outlet or with a connector.

○ Using the wrong plug in the wrong receptacle or use of a worn fixture can cause fire and corrosion problems.

○ The lamp takes a 60 watt bulb and is fitted with a 13 amp plug.

pole piece /pəʊl pis/ (pole pieces)

ELECTRICAL POWER: MOTOR OR GENERATOR

NOUN A **pole piece** is a piece of magnetic material that forms an extension of the magnetic circuit in an electric motor, and is used to concentrate the magnetic field where it will be most effective.

○ *The current in the rotor creates a magnetic flux that reacts with the pole piece to create torque.*

○ *When the current of the AC wave form increases from zero toward its positive peak, a magnetic field is created in the pole piece.*

pol|y|phase /pɒlɪfeɪz/

CIRCUITS / ELECTRICAL POWER / COMPUTING AND CONTROL

ADJECTIVE A **polyphase** electrical system, circuit, or device has, generates, or uses two or more alternating voltages of the same frequency, whose phases are cyclically displaced by fractions of a period.

○ *Installations can reduce the stroboscope effect by operating the lamps on different phases of a polyphase power supply.*

○ *A polyphase transmission line requires less conductor material than a single-phase line for transmitting the same amount of power at the same voltage.*

port /pɔrt/ (ports)

COMPUTING AND CONTROL

NOUN A **port** is a pair of terminals through which a single current may enter or leave a network.

○ *The device includes a USB power port that's perfect for powering wireless adapters to stream your music wirelessly from your computer or iPod.*

○ *A three terminal component effectively has two (or more) ports and the transfer function cannot be expressed as a single impedance.*

port|a|ble e|quip|ment /pɔrtəbəl ɪkwɪpmənt/

CIRCUITS / ELECTRICAL POWER / COMPUTING AND CONTROL

NOUN **Portable equipment** is electrical equipment that can easily be moved from one place to another while in operation or while connected to the supply.

○ *Battery life has become a key selling feature of portable equipment, as users can expect today's system to operate for a much longer time than one purchased just two years ago.*

○ *Lithium-ion cells are very popular for portable equipment such as notebook computers, video cameras, and cell phones.*

---

pos|i|tive feed|back /pɒzɪtɪv fi̱dbæk/

COMPUTING AND CONTROL

NOUN **Positive feedback** is feedback where the returning signal improves the effect of the input signal.

○ *The howl in an audio system which happens when the microphone is too near the speakers, is caused by positive feedback.*

○ *The echo suppressor is an active device used by the phone company to suppress positive feedback on the phone network.*

---

po|ten|tial dif|fer|ence (ABBR **PD**) /pətɛ̱nʃ°l di̱fərəns/

GENERAL

NOUN **Potential difference** is the work done in moving a unit of positive electric charge from one point to another. The symbol for potential difference is V.

○ *If you connect the two ends of the same wire to opposite ends of the same battery, current will flow through it due to the potential difference between the two ends of the battery.*

○ *Ohm's law states that the current through a conductor between two points is directly proportional to the potential difference or voltage across the two points.*

---

po|ten|ti|om|e|ter /pətɛ̱nʃi̱ɒmɪtər/ (**potentiometers**)

ELECTRONICS COMPONENTS

NOUN A **potentiometer** is a variable resistor in which a wiper sweeps from one end of the resistive element to the other, resulting in resistance that is proportional to the wiper's position.

○ *These variable resistors are known as potentiometers when all three terminals are present, since they act as a continuously adjustable voltage divider.*

○ *Digital potentiometers are versatile devices that you can use in many filtering and waveform-generation applications.*

pow|er /paʊər/

NOUN **Power** is electricity obtained in large quantities from a fuel source that is used to operate machines, lights, and heating.

○ We need to calculate the power consumption of this system in watts.

○ Should the wind turbine produce more power than the demand of the house, this excess power is fed into the grid via a meter that counts the units fed into the grid.

TALKING ABOUT POWER

We usually say that power is **generated** or **produced** when it is made.

A thing or process that power comes from is a **source** of power.

A power **failure** or **outage** is a temporary loss of electric power to an area.

---

pow|er fac|tor (ABBR **PF**) /paʊər fæktər/ (**power factors**)

NOUN A **power factor** is the ratio of the active power consumed by a component or circuit to the apparent power.

○ In the context of electrical power, capacitor banks are used to correct lagging power factor on distribution and transmission systems to allow the most efficient use of those facilities.

○ Power factor is defined as the ratio of the average power in an AC circuit to the apparent power, which is the product of the voltage and current magnitudes.

---

pow|er fac|tor cor|rec|tion (ABBR **PFC**) /paʊər fæktər kərɛkʃən/

NOUN **Power factor correction** is the process of increasing the power factor to near unity without altering the original load.

○ The power factor of a network is a measure of how efficiently the power is used and power factor correction is technology and equipment used to ensure this is as efficient as possible.

○ *In order to eliminate line losses, the power factor correction device must be mounted at the inductive load.*

---

pow|er grid /paʊər grɪd/ (power grids)

ELECTRICAL POWER: DISTRIBUTION

NOUN A **power grid** is a network of power lines and associated equipment used to transmit and distribute electricity over a geographic area.

○ *Two (or more) inductors that have coupled magnetic flux form a transformer, which is a fundamental component of every electric utility power grid.*

○ *Distributed generation permits the consumer who is generating heat or electricity for their own needs to send their surplus electrical power back into the power grid.*

---

pow|er line /paʊər laɪn/ (power lines)

ELECTRICAL POWER: DISTRIBUTION

NOUN A **power line** is a set of conductors used to transmit and distribute electrical energy.

○ *When lightning strikes a power line, the damaging effects are felt throughout the grid, even miles away.*

○ *The apparatus has a power supply with at least two input terminals, including a first input terminal coupled to the conductive body and a second input terminal coupled to the power line.*

---

pow|er plant /paʊər plænt/ (power plants)

ELECTRICAL POWER

NOUN A **power plant** is the equipment supplying power to a particular machine or for a particular operation or process.

○ *Generally, a conventional power plant emits the heat created as a by-product of electricity generation into the environment through cooling towers, as flue gas, or by other means.*

○ *Generally, a conventional power plant emits the heat created as a by-product of electricity generation into the environment through cooling towers, as flue gas, or by other means.*

pow|er point /paʊər pɔɪnt/ (**power points**)

ELECTRICAL POWER: POWER CONSUMPTION

NOUN A **power point** is an electrical socket on a wall.

○ If you want to disconnect the device, switch off the switch at the power point and wait for 10 seconds before disconnecting the 3-pin plug to allow for power to dissipate.

○ For safety's sake never operate any mains powered electric devices with a residual current device installed between the machine and the mains power point.

pow|er sta|tion /paʊər steɪʃən/ (**power stations**)

ELECTRICAL POWER: GENERATION

NOUN A **power station** is an electrical generating station.

○ The use of transformers has allowed power to be generated in isolation and supplied across larger distances, which means that society can have electricity from one main power station rather than many.

○ Alternators in central power station use may also control the field current to regulate reactive power and to help stabilize the power system against the effects of momentary faults.

pow|er sup|ply /paʊər səplaɪ/ (**power supplies**)

CIRCUITS / ELECTRICAL POWER / COMPUTING AND CONTROL

NOUN The **power supply** of a circuit is the part that supplies power to the entire circuit or part of the circuit.

○ Capacitors are commonly used in electronic devices to maintain power supply while batteries are being changed.

○ When switching the voltage output, it is best to temporarily switch the power supply off and then restart.

pri|ma|ry wind|ing /praɪmɛri waɪndɪŋ/ (**primary windings**)

CIRCUITS / ELECTRICAL POWER / COMPUTING AND CONTROL

NOUN A **primary winding** is the winding of a transformer that is connected to and receives energy from an external source of electrons.

○ A transformer is an electromagnetic device that has a primary winding and a secondary winding that transfer energy from one electrical circuit to another by magnetic coupling without moving parts.

○ The primary winding is analogous to the input shaft and the secondary winding to the output shaft.

---

print|ed cir|cuit board (ABBR **PCB**) /ˈprɪntɪd ˈsɜːrkɪt bɔːrd/ (**printed circuit boards**)

SEMICONDUCTOR AND ELECTRONIC CIRCUITRY

NOUN A **printed circuit board** is a non-conductive material with conductive lines on it, onto which electronic components can be mounted and connected by traces to form a working circuit or assembly.

○ Several capacitors could be mounted on the printed circuit board, in ratios of five or ten, and switched in for different operating voltages.

○ Modern printed circuit boards are multi-layer with surface components being mounted by machine.

---

push but|ton /pʊʃ ˈbʌtən/ (**push buttons**)

GENERAL

NOUN A **push button** is an electrical switch operated by pressing a button, that closes or opens a circuit.

○ When a push button is pressed, it makes contact with an extension which in turn makes contact with the gold-plated surface of the circuit edge.

○ When contact is made between an extension displaced by a push button and the circuit, the contact closes a circuit switch within the circuit.

---

py|lon /ˈpaɪlɒn/ (**pylons**)

ELECTRICAL POWER: DISTRIBUTION

NOUN A **pylon** is a large vertical steel tower-like structure that supports high-tension electrical cables.

○ Because power lines are typically 400,000 volts, and ground is at an electrical potential voltage of zero volts, pylons create electric fields between the cables they carry and the ground.

○ Overhead line insulators are used to electrically insulate pylons from live electrical cables.

Qq

Q fac|tor /kyu fæktər/ (Q factors) (short for quality factor)

NOUN The **Q factor** of certain electrical components and devices is a measure of the relationship between stored energy and the rate of energy use, that gives an indication of their efficiency.

- ○ *The higher the Q factor of the inductor, the closer it approaches the behavior of an ideal, lossless, inductor.*

- ○ *If you are deliberately using the inductor as part of a resonant circuit, then it is important to note that the Q factor of a self resonant circuit is generally not high.*

▶ **SYNONYM:**
damping factor

q

Rr

ra|di|an (ABBR rad) /reɪdiən/ (radians)

GENERAL

NOUN The **radian** is the plane angle between two radii of a circle that cut off on the circumference an arc equal in length to the radius.

○ The radian is the standard unit of angular measure, used in many areas of mathematics.

○ Since radians are a unit-less measurement the normalized angular frequency is sometimes referred to as inverse samples.

ra|di|o /reɪdiou/

COMMUNICATION

NOUN **Radio** is the use of electromagnetic radiation to communicate electrical signals without wires, to create sound broadcasting, television, and radar.

○ When used in the context of radio, MHz refers to the number of oscillations of electromagnetic radiation per second.

○ The magnitude of transfer function is called amplitude response or frequency response especially in radio applications.

rat|ing /reɪtɪŋ/

ELECTRICAL POWER

NOUN The **rating** of an electrical device tells you what current, frequency, and voltage it is designed for.

○ Another practical use of a power attenuator would be to reduce the power of an amplifier to match the power rating of the speaker.

○ You need to specify the voltage and current ratings of both windings in each transformer for each of the connections.

re|ac|tance /riˈæktəns/

CIRCUITS / ELECTRICAL POWER / COMPUTING AND CONTROL

NOUN **Reactance** is a form of opposition that electronic components exhibit to the passage of alternating current because of capacitance or inductance.

○ *The speaker's reactance does not play a part in shaping the overall tone, since the interaction between the speaker and the tube amplifier is non-existent.*

○ *You can determine the leakage reactance of each winding on the basis that the same amount of equivalent leakage flux links each winding.*

re|ac|tive pow|er /riˈæktɪv paʊər/

CIRCUITS / ELECTRICAL POWER

NOUN **Reactive power** is the part of complex power that corresponds to storage and retrieval of energy rather than consumption.

○ *On an AC power system, there are two kinds of power – real power that actually does work, and reactive power that enables transformers to transform, generators to generate, and motors to rotate.*

○ *Capacitors can be used to intercept the reactive power from inductive motors, and return it to the source on the next cycle.*

re|ceiv|er /rɪˈsiːvər/ (**receivers**)

COMMUNICATION

NOUN A **receiver** is a circuit that accepts signals from a transmission medium and decodes or translates them into a form that can drive local circuits. The symbol for a receiver is Rx.

○ *A receiver tuned to the frequency of radio waves can amplify and decode them and reproduce the sound that was encoded on them at the station.*

○ *The circuit cuts off receiver output when no input signal is being received.*

rec|ti|fi|ca|tion /ˌrɛktɪfɪˈkeɪʃən/

CIRCUITS / ELECTRICAL POWER / COMPUTING AND CONTROL

NOUN **Rectification** is the conversion of alternating current to pulsating direct current.

○ *Full-wave rectification converts both polarities of the input waveform to direct current, and is more efficient.*

○ *The smoothing reactors are provided to remove the AC ripple which is left over from the rectification cycle.*

---

rec|ti|fi|er /rɛktɪfaɪər/ (**rectifiers**)

CIRCUITS / ELECTRICAL POWER / COMPUTING AND CONTROL

NOUN A **rectifier** is a device that converts alternating current to pulsating direct current.

○ *Virtually all electronic devices require DC, so rectifiers find uses inside the power supplies of virtually all electronic equipment.*

○ *Most automotive applications use DC although the generator is an AC device which uses a rectifier to produce DC.*

---

rec|ti|fy /rɛktɪfaɪ/ (**rectifies, rectified, rectifying**)

CIRCUITS / ELECTRICAL POWER / COMPUTING AND CONTROL

VERB If a device **rectifies** current, it converts alternating current into direct current.

○ *When the alternating current supply is rectified to obtain the direct current needed by most electronics, the current waveform may be far from sinusoidal.*

○ *In order to produce steady DC from a rectified AC supply, a smoothing circuit or filter is required.*

---

reg|u|la|tion /rɛgyəleɪʃ°n/

ELECTRICAL POWER: POWER CONSUMPTION

NOUN **Regulation** is the change in voltage that occurs when a load is connected across a power supply, caused by internal resistance or impedance.

○ *The stabilizer accepts a wide range of input voltage while maintaining tight voltage regulation and has a high momentary overload capacity for demanding applications.*

○ *If the output voltage is too high, the regulation element will normally be commanded to produce a lower voltage.*

---

re|lay /rileɪ/ (**relays**)

CIRCUITS / ELECTRICAL POWER / COMPUTING AND CONTROL

NOUN A **relay** is an electromagnetic switching device that consists of an armature that is moved by an electromagnet to operate one or more switch contacts.

○ *Electromechanical relays comprise one or more electrical contacts having a mechanical movement, these being coupled to a moveable element of the magnetic circuit of an electromagnet.*

○ *When the main current exceeds the specification, the output voltage of the current transformer activates the relay and the protective circuit.*

---

re|luc|tance /rɪlʌktəns/

CIRCUITS / ELECTRICAL POWER / COMPUTING AND CONTROL

NOUN The **reluctance** of a magnetic material is its ability to oppose the flow of magnetic flux.

○ *The magnetic flux created by the field windings follows the path of least magnetic reluctance.*

○ *An excessive current may be due to a partial short circuit between one or more turns in the winding or it may be due to some defects in the magnetic circuit which alter the reluctance of the core.*

---

re|mote con|trol /rɪməʊt kəntrəʊl/

COMPUTING AND CONTROL

NOUN **Remote control** is a way of controlling an electrical device from a distance.

○ *The remote control supplied makes it possible to hide the unit away in a corner if need be and still offer easy operation from a distance.*

○ *With a click of a button on your remote control, you can make selections and choices from on-screen menus.*

---

re|new|a|ble en|er|gy /rɪnu̯əbəl ɛnərdʒi/

ELECTRICAL POWER: GENERATION

NOUN **Renewable energy** is energy from energy sources that are derived from the sun, wind, or other natural processes, and that are always available.

○ *Some people say that renewable energy sources are not sufficient to meet the world's energy requirements without fossil fuels, and that nuclear power must be part of the mix.*

○ With today's heavy focus on clean, renewable energy sources and the desire to reduce carbon footprints, solar energy will likely be an energy source of choice for many.

re|peat|er /rɪpiːtər/ (repeaters)

COMPUTING AND CONTROL

NOUN A **repeater** is a device that amplifies or adds to incoming electrical signals and retransmits them, in order to compensate for transmission losses.

○ A repeater receives a signal and retransmits it at a higher level or higher power, or onto the other side of an obstruction, so that the signal can cover longer distances.

○ A repeater is used to boost the serial communications signal strength for long cable runs.

re|sid|u|al cur|rent de|vice /rɪzɪdʒuəl kɜrənt dɪvaɪs/ (residual current devices)

ELECTRICAL POWER: POWER CONSUMPTION

NOUN A **residual current device** is a device in electrical equipment that will break the circuit in order to protect the person using it from electrocution.

○ A residual current device disconnects a circuit whenever it detects that the flow of current is not balanced between the phase conductor and the neutral conductor.

○ The residual current device is used to detect ground fault currents and to interrupt supply if a ground current flows.

re|sist|ance (ABBR **R**) /rɪzɪstəns/

CIRCUITS / ELECTRICAL POWER / COMPUTING AND CONTROL

NOUN **Resistance** is a measure of the opposition to electrical flow in DC systems, counted in ohms.

○ As batteries age and fail, their internal resistance will typically increase because the plate surface can sulfate or shed active material, which adversely affects its ability to perform.

○ DC resistance will limit the amount of direct current the device can carry without overheating, or without saturating.

re|sis|tive /rɪzɪstɪv/

CIRCUITS / ELECTRICAL POWER / COMPUTING AND CONTROL

ADJECTIVE **Resistive** material shows electrical resistance.

○ A terminator is a resistive load placed at the end of a cable to prevent data signals from reflecting back into the data path.

○ A resistive load is a resistor that is measured in ohms and is always the same regardless of the signal voltage across it, AC or DC.

▶ **COLLOCATIONS:**
resistive circuit
resistive load
resistive wire

res|o|nance /rɛzənəns/

SEMICONDUCTOR AND ELECTRONIC CIRCUITRY: ANALOG

NOUN **Resonance** is a condition in a circuit in which the size of the voltage or the current becomes a maximum or the circuit becomes purely resistive.

○ Electrical resonance occurs in an electric circuit at a particular resonant frequency when the impedance of the circuit is at a minimum in a series circuit or at a maximum in a parallel circuit.

○ At frequencies below resonance, capacitive current will decrease; above the resonant frequency, inductive current will decrease.

res|o|nant cir|cuit /rɛzənənt sɜrkɪt/ (**resonant circuits**)

SEMICONDUCTOR AND ELECTRONIC CIRCUITRY: ANALOG

NOUN A **resonant circuit** combines an inductor and capacitor to make a circuit that responds to a frequency.

○ Because filters are made from inductors and capacitors, they are resonant circuits and their performance and resonance can depend critically on their source and load impedances.

○ The oscillating waveform will have a dampening trail due to the natural resistance of the resonant circuit.

▶ **SYNONYMS:**
LC circuit
tuned circuit

r

re|sponse time /rɪspɒns taɪm/ (**response times**)

COMPUTING AND CONTROL

NOUN The **response time** of a sensor is the time it takes for it to respond from no load to a sudden change in load.

○ The thermocouple has a much faster response time and so gives a more representative indication of the heating element temperature.

○ In fuel cells, the electrical response time of the power section is fast, as it is associated with the speed at which the chemical reaction can restore the charge that has been drained by the load.

R|F /ɑr ɛf/ (short for **radio frequency**)

COMMUNICATION

ABBREVIATION RF is a term used to describe the range of frequencies that are suitable to be transmitted through the air without wires.

○ Unlicensed RF bands are particularly challenging with no ability to control noisy neighboring networks.

○ Most electronic devices incorporate an RF inductor.

R|F|I /ɑr ɛf aɪ/ (short for **radio-frequency interference**)

COMMUNICATION

ABBREVIATION RFI is unwanted noise from RF sources.

○ The attenuator is especially useful in applications where balanced audio devices near strong RFI sources, such as AM radio stations, are connected by long cable runs.

○ Improve the performance of every component in your audio/video system by reducing RFI that comes with the main AC line.

rhe|o|stat /riːəstæt/ (**rheostats**)

CIRCUITS / ELECTRICAL POWER

NOUN A **rheostat** is an electrical instrument used to vary resistance, that usually consists of a coil of wire with a terminal at one end and a sliding contact that moves along the coil to stop the current.

○ Sometimes a rheostat is made from resistance wire wound on a heat-resisting cylinder with the slider made from a number of metal fingers that grip lightly onto some of the turns of resistance wire.

○ *Since the field rheostat is normally set to minimum resistance, the speed of the motor will not be excessive.*

ring cir|cuit /rɪŋ sɜrkɪt/ (ring circuits)

ELECTRICAL POWER: POWER CONSUMPTION

NOUN A **ring circuit** is an electrical system in which distribution points are connected to the main supply in a continuous closed circuit.

○ *To rewire your house, make sure you are using the correct gauge wire for each ring circuit, such as lights, sockets, showers, and cookers.*

○ *The ring circuit may be some kilometers in length and secondary distribution substations can be situated at various points around the ring.*

ring main /rɪŋ meɪn/ (ring mains)

ELECTRICAL POWER: POWER CONSUMPTION

NOUN A **ring main** is a domestic electrical supply in which outlet sockets are connected to the mains supply through a ring circuit.

○ *Once the faulted circuit has been located, it can be isolated and grounded, via the ring main units, to allow safe repair work.*

○ *The ring main starts at the consumer unit and returns to the consumer unit.*

rip|ple /rɪpᵊl/ (ripples)

CIRCUITS / ELECTRICAL POWER

NOUN A **ripple** is a fluctuation in the intensity of a steady current or voltage.

○ *Inductors are very useful for filtering out residual ripple in a power supply.*

○ *The detector may start to track the amplitude modulation in the signal and thereby distort the amplitude information as well as introduce excess ripple on the gain control signal.*

R|M|S /ɑr ɛm ɛs/ (short for **root-mean-square**)

CIRCUITS / ELECTRICAL POWER / COMPUTING AND CONTROL

ABBREVIATION The **RMS** value of a periodic waveform is the same as the effective value of the waveform, and is obtained by taking the square root of the mean of the squared waveform.

○ *Anytime you hear about a voltage value for your house wiring or somewhere on the power grid, you can safely assume the value is in RMS form.*

○ *The RMS voltage is proportional to the temperature of the resistor and how resistive it is.*

ROM /rɒm/ (short for **read-only memory**)

SEMICONDUCTOR AND ELECTRONIC CIRCUITRY

ABBREVIATION ROM is the permanent part of a computer's memory, where stored information can be read but not changed.

○ *The monitor program of a single-board microcomputer is generally stored in the ROM.*

○ *The processor's ROM is programmed with preset information that is permanently programmed with core functions in order to facilitate processor communication with the data bus.*

---

ro|tor /roʊtər/ (**rotors**)

ELECTRICAL POWER: MOTOR OR GENERATOR

NOUN A rotor is the rotating cylindrical part of a machine, placed inside the stator with a narrow air gap in between to allow for smooth rotation.

○ *The rotor consists of a multi-pole electromagnet which induces output voltage in the stator of the generator when it is rotated by the engine.*

○ *It is possible to rotate the rotor with very high speeds of 20–30 thousand revolutions per minute, and this high rotational speed provides for a high output voltage.*

---

r|p|m /ɑr pi ɛm/ (short for **revs per minute**)

CIRCUITS / ELECTRICAL POWER

ABBREVIATION Rpm is the speed of rotation of a machine expressed in revolutions per minute.

○ *The drum rotates at a speed between 400 and 700 rpm.*

○ *If the speed is 4000 rpm, the induction motor will act as an asynchronous generator.*

Ss

---

sche|mat|ic /skimǽtɪk/ (schematics)

NOUN A **schematic** is a schematic diagram of an electrical circuit.

○ As shown in the schematic, the output current is the current flowing through R2.

○ After reviewing the schematic it is evident that the low speed supply conductors carry current in the high-speed connection.

---

se|cond (ABBR **s**) /sɛkənd/ (seconds)

NOUN A **second** is a unit of time, and one of the sixty parts that a minute is divided into.

○ In North America, electricity is generated at 60 Hz, which means that the electrons move forward, then back again, 60 times in one second.

○ If the power comes from an alternating-current source like in most of today's homes and offices in the United States, the poles will switch places 60 times a second.

---

s

sec|ond|ar|y wind|ing /sɛkəndɛri waɪndɪŋ/ (secondary windings)

NOUN A **secondary winding** is the winding of a transformer that receives its energy by electromagnetic induction from the primary winding.

○ The secondary winding is facilitated with larger-gauge wire because of the increase in current, whereas the primary winding is made up of smaller-gauge wire due to less current conduction.

○ The electromotive force in the secondary winding, if connected to an electrical circuit, will cause current to flow in the secondary circuit.

RELATED WORDS

Compare **secondary winding** with **primary winding**, which is the winding of a transformer that is connected to and receives energy from an external source of electrons.

---

sem|i|con|duc|tor /sɛmikəndʌktər/ (**semiconductors**)

SEMICONDUCTOR AND ELECTRONIC CIRCUITRY

NOUN A **semiconductor** is a substance that can act as an electrical conductor or insulator depending on chemical alterations or external conditions.

○ *Air, glass, most plastics, and rubber are insulators, and then there are some materials called semiconductors, that seem to be good conductors sometimes but much less so at other times.*

○ *Semiconductors such as germanium and silicon are neither conductors nor insulators of electricity, but possess unique electrical properties that make them excellent signal detectors.*

---

se|ries /sɪəriz/ (**series**)

CIRCUITS / ELECTRICAL POWER

NOUN Two or more elements are connected **in series** if they are connected one after the other with the same current passing through them.

○ *Two resistors, of value 7.3 ohm and 4.2 ohm are connected in series with a 24 volts battery.*

○ *If the four light bulbs are connected in series, there is the same current flowing through all of them.*

---

se|ries mo|tor /sɪəriz moʊtər/ (**series motors**)

ELECTRICAL POWER: MOTOR OR GENERATOR

NOUN A **series motor** is a direct current motor that has two windings that are in series, with the same current flowing through each.

○ *Use of series motors is generally limited to cases where a heavy power demand is necessary to bring the machine up to speed, as in the case of certain elevator and hoist installations.*

○ *The series motor provides high starting torque and is able to move very large shaft loads when it is first energized.*

se|ries res|o|nance /sɪəriz rɛzənəns/

SEMICONDUCTOR AND ELECTRONIC CIRCUITRY: ANALOG

NOUN **Series resonance** is a resonance condition that usually occurs in series circuits, where the current becomes a maximum for a particular voltage.

○ In series resonance, the current is maximum at resonant frequency.

○ The series resonance current curve increases to a maximum at resonance then decreases as resonance is passed.

se|ries-wound /sɪərizwaʊnd/

ELECTRICAL POWER: MOTOR OR GENERATOR

ADJECTIVE If a motor or generator is **series-wound**, it has the field and armature circuits connected in series.

○ An inductor and a power resistor are placed in series to simulate the resistance and inductance of a large series-wound DC motor.

○ The series-wound generator is used principally to supply a constant current at variable voltage.

RELATED WORDS

Compare **series-wound** with **shunt-wound** in which the motor or generator has the field and armature circuits connected in parallel.

---

ser|vo /sɜrvoʊ/

COMPUTING AND CONTROL

ADJECTIVE If equipment or devices are **servo**, they relate to, form part of, or are operated by a servomechanism.

○ A servo motor is a motor, very often sold as a complete module, which is used within a position-control or speed-control feedback control system.

○ A servo motor is an electromechanical device in which an electrical input determines the position of the armature of a motor.

ser|vo|mech|a|nism /sɜrvoumɛkənɪzəm/
(**servomechanisms**)

COMPUTING AND CONTROL

NOUN A **servomechanism** is a mechanical or electromechanical system for control of the position or speed of an output transducer.

○ *If the output voltage is not in the acceptable range, the servomechanism switches connections or moves the wiper to adjust the voltage into the acceptable region.*

○ *The voltage stabilizer uses a servomechanism to control the position of the tap (or wiper) of the autotransformer, usually with a motor.*

shield|ing /ʃildɪŋ/

CIRCUITS / ELECTRICAL POWER / COMPUTING AND CONTROL

NOUN **Shielding** is the process of protecting pieces of equipment from the effect of electrostatic fields that are external to the equipment itself.

○ *These instruments are free from external magnetic field influences because of magnetic shielding.*

○ *The effective protection or shielding given by the ground wire depends on the height of the ground wire above the ground.*

short cir|cuit /ʃɔrt sɜrkɪt/ (**short circuits**)

CIRCUITS / ELECTRICAL POWER / COMPUTING AND CONTROL

NOUN A **short circuit** is a situation in which a faulty connection or damaged wire causes electricity to travel along the wrong route and damage an electrical device.

○ *If the hot wire should ever accidentally touch the case, a short circuit would blow the fuses in the building and quickly remove the electrical connections, and the hazard.*

○ *A short circuit is generally an unintended electrical connection between current carrying parts.*

short cir|cuit cur|rent /ʃɔrt sɜrkɪt kɜrənt/ (**short circuit currents**)

CIRCUITS / ELECTRICAL POWER

NOUN A **short circuit current** is an overcurrent resulting from a short circuit.

S

○ If the short circuit current is excessive, then the electrolyte will heat up and either leak or cause the capacitor to explode.

○ With the ground connection the current would flow through the ground line back to the power source, and this short circuit current would cause the system circuit breaker to trip.

---

shunt /ʃʌnt/ (**shunts**)

ELECTRICAL POWER: MOTOR OR GENERATOR

NOUN A **shunt** is any component connected in parallel. A current shunt is a device for altering the amount of electric current flowing through a piece of apparatus, such as a galvanometer.

○ A shunt generator is a method in which field winding and armature winding are connected in parallel, and in which the armature supplies both the load current and the field current.

○ A current shunt is a device for altering the amount of electric current flowing through a piece of apparatus, such as a galvanometer.

---

shunt mo|tor /ʃʌnt moʊtər/ (**shunt motors**)

ELECTRICAL POWER: MOTOR OR GENERATOR

NOUN A **shunt motor** is a direct current motor whose two windings are in parallel, with the same voltage across each.

○ For a shunt motor, induced voltage is proportional to speed, and torque is proportional to armature current.

○ A shunt motor is designed to run at practically constant speed, regardless of the load.

---

shunt-wound /ʃʌntwaʊnd/

ELECTRICAL POWER: MOTOR OR GENERATOR

ADJECTIVE A **shunt-wound** motor or generator has the field and armature circuits connected in parallel.

○ Current in the field windings of a shunt-wound generator is independent of the load current, because currents in parallel branches are independent of each other.

○ A shunt-wound generator is wired differently than a series-wound generator, and its voltage output performs in an opposite way: As the load increases, the voltage output decreases.

S

shut|down /ˈʃʌtdaʊn/

SEMICONDUCTOR AND ELECTRONIC CIRCUITRY

NOUN **Shutdown** is a process that takes place in many integrated circuits, that greatly reduces power consumption when the device is not in use.

○ Short circuits, voltage overload, and output overload all result in automatic shutdown.

○ The auto shutdown will kick in when the unit gets too hot.

sie|mens (ABBR **S**) /ˈsiːmənz/ (**siemens**)

GENERAL

NOUN A **siemens** is a unit of electric conductance equal to the conductance between two points of a conductor having a resistance of 1 watt.

○ A dielectric is a nonconductor of electricity, especially a substance with electrical conductivity of less than a millionth of a siemens.

○ The SI unit of electrical resistance is the ohm, and its reciprocal quantity is electrical conductance measured in siemens.

sig|nal /ˈsɪɡnəl/ (**signals**)

CIRCUITS / COMMUNICATION / COMPUTING AND CONTROL

NOUN A **signal** is a series of radio waves or changes in electrical current that may carry information.

○ An amp that uses a fixed current source of 2.5A from the positive supply will draw 2.5A regardless of load or signal level, but only from the positive supply.

○ A filter changes the amplitude or phase characteristics of a signal with respect to frequency.

sine wave /ˈsaɪn weɪv/ (**sine waves**)

CIRCUITS / COMMUNICATION / COMPUTING AND CONTROL

NOUN A **sine wave** is the fundamental waveform from which other waveforms may be generated.

○ The voltage and current waveforms produced from the power company generators are basic sine waves.

○ The peak-to-peak value is twice the maximum or peak value of the sine wave and is sometimes used for measurement of AC voltages.

sin|gle-phase /sɪŋgəl feɪz/

CIRCUITS / ELECTRICAL POWER

ADJECTIVE A **single-phase** system, circuit, or device has, generates, or uses a single alternating voltage.

○ Single-phase electric power refers to the distribution of alternating current electric power using a system in which all the voltages of the supply vary in unison.

○ In electrical engineering, single-phase electric power refers to the distribution of electric power using a system in which all the voltages of the supply vary in unison.

RELATED WORDS

Compare **single-phase** with **three-phase**, which means having, generating, or using three alternating voltages of the same frequency.

---

si|nus|oid /saɪnəsɔɪd/ (**sinusoids**)

CIRCUITS / ELECTRICAL POWER

NOUN A **sinusoid** is a signal that has a form of a sine wave.

○ The shape of the supply voltage for power distribution is known as a sinusoid as it resembles a sine or cosine waveshape.

○ The only true way to get a pure sine wave is to use a motor generator set where you use the DC power to run a DC motor which then runs an AC alternator producing true sinusoid waveforms.

---

skin ef|fect /skɪn ɪfɛkt/

COMMUNICATION

NOUN **Skin effect** is the tendency of current to stick to the outer layers of a conductor due to the presence of internal flux, that often happens at higher frequencies.

○ The single biggest source of distortion in electrical transmission lines is the skin effect, which causes a dramatic increase in the effective resistance of the conductors as frequency increases.

○ At short-wave frequencies, a phenomenon named skin effect forces all current to flow into the outside layer of metal.

slip /slɪp/

ELECTRICAL POWER: MOTOR OR GENERATOR

NOUN **Slip** is the per unit speed by which the rotor falls behind the stator field.

○ The difference between the motor speed and the output speed is called the slip speed.

○ In induction motors there has to be slip between the rotor and stator to create rotor current for producing the field.

slip ring /slɪp rɪŋ/ (slip rings)

ELECTRICAL POWER: MOTOR OR GENERATOR

NOUN A **slip ring** is a metal ring, mounted on but insulated from a rotating shaft of a motor or generator, by means of which current can be led through stationary brushes into or out of a winding on the shaft.

○ State of the art wind turbine systems use contacting brush and slip ring mechanisms to facilitate power transfer between the stator and the rotor.

○ The inverter includes a single or pair of resonant circuits that are connected to the slip ring either directly or through a transformer.

sock|et /sɒkɪt/ (sockets)

GENERAL

NOUN A **socket** is a device into which an electric plug can be inserted in order to make a connection in a circuit.

○ In the US, the average voltage in household wall sockets is about 120V and it changes 60 times per second.

○ Simply plug the device into the microphone socket and press the record button.

so|lar cell /soʊlər sɛl/ (solar cells)

ELECTRONICS COMPONENTS

NOUN A **solar cell** is a device that converts energy from the sun directly into electrical energy.

○ A solar cell is a source of electricity which gets electrical energy from light energy.

○ A solar cell generates electricity from light.

so|lar pan|el /ˈsoʊlər pænᵊl/ (**solar panels**)

SEMICONDUCTOR AND ELECTRONIC CIRCUITRY

NOUN A **solar panel** is a panel exposed to radiation from the sun, that is used to heat water or, when mounted with solar cells, to produce electricity.

○ The solar panel charges a battery during the day that powers our proprietary light bulbs which automatically come on via a light sensor and timer system at night.

○ The solar panel has high efficiency crystalline solar cells, and is easy to install and completely maintenance free.

so|lar pow|er /ˈsoʊlər paʊər/

ELECTRICAL POWER: GENERATION

NOUN **Solar power** is heat radiation from the sun that is converted into electrical power.

○ With a solar power setup, you can generate free power anywhere the sun shines even in remote locations.

○ For recreational vehicles, solar power provides the freedom to go to more remote locations, without relying on a plug-in power source or a noisy electric generator.

so|le|noid /ˈsoʊlɪnɔɪd/ (**solenoids**)

CIRCUITS / ELECTRICAL POWER / COMPUTING AND CONTROL

NOUN A **solenoid** is a coil of wire wound on a cylinder, that has a length that is large compared with its radius.

○ A solenoid is a long, thin loop of wire, often wrapped around a metallic core, which produces a magnetic field when an electric current is passed through it.

○ Domestic coffee machines use an inlet water hose which is triggered by a solenoid to fill up the water reservoir whenever needed.

sol|id-state /ˈsɒlɪd steɪt/

SEMICONDUCTOR AND ELECTRONIC CIRCUITRY

ADJECTIVE A **solid-state** device or circuit is one that relies on semiconductors rather than mechanical or vacuum tube circuits.

○ The relay is a single-pole, normally open, solid-state replacement for electromechanical relays used for general purpose switching of analog signals.

○*A solid-state thermoelectric generator device can directly drive a high voltage grid at voltage without a special step-up transformer.*

---

square wave /skwɛər weɪv/ (**square waves**)

SEMICONDUCTOR AND ELECTRONIC CIRCUITRY

NOUN A **square wave** is a periodic wave that alternates between two fixed amplitudes for equal lengths of time.

○*A square wave starts at one of two extreme voltages, not the mid point.*

○*A control for a voltage fed series resonant inverter includes controllable switch means which supplies square wave voltage signals to a resonant series circuit.*

---

squir|rel cage /skwɜrəl keɪdʒ/ (**squirrel cages**)

ELECTRICAL POWER: MOTOR OR GENERATOR

NOUN A **squirrel cage** is the rotor of an induction motor with a cylindrical winding with copper bars around the edge parallel to the axis.

○*At low speeds, the current induced in the squirrel cage is nearly at line frequency and tends to be in the outer parts of the rotor cage.*

○*The squirrel cage rotor has a ring at either end of the rotor, with bars connecting the rings running the length of the rotor.*

---

star con|nec|tion /stɑr kənɛkʃən/ (**star connections**)

ELECTRICAL POWER

NOUN A **star connection** is a connection used in a polyphase electrical device or system of devices in which the windings each have one end connected to a common junction, and the other end to a separate terminal.

○*The line voltage is applied to one end of each of the three windings, with the other end bridged together, effectively connecting the windings in a star connection.*

○*The power transformer has a delta connection in the primary winding and a star connection in the secondary winding.*

start|er /stɑrtər/ (**starters**)

ELECTRICAL POWER: MOTOR OR GENERATOR

NOUN A **starter** is a machine that helps the starting process of an electrical device.

○ *If a starter solenoid receives insufficient power from the battery, it will fail to start the motor.*

○ *An autotransformer starter uses an autotransformer to reduce the voltage applied to a motor during start.*

sta|tor /steɪtər/ (**stators**)

ELECTRICAL POWER: MOTOR OR GENERATOR

NOUN A **stator** is the stationary part of a machine in the form of a hollow cylinder inside which the rotor will be placed with a narrow air gap between them.

○ *The development of electric motors of acceptable efficiency was delayed for several decades by failure to recognize the extreme importance of a relatively small air gap between rotor and stator.*

○ *The main electrical elements of our motors are the stator, in which the exciter winding is included, and the rotor.*

stead|y-state re|sponse /stɛdi steɪt rɪspɒns/ (**steady-state responses**)

COMPUTING AND CONTROL

NOUN A **steady-state response** is the behavior of a circuit after a long time when steady conditions have been reached after an external excitation.

○ *The transient response is from the time the switch is flipped until the output reaches a steady 5 volts, and at this time the power supply reaches its steady-state response of a constant 5 volts.*

○ *The poles and zeros will control the steady-state response at any given frequency.*

> **RELATED WORDS**
>
> Compare **steady-state response** with **transient response**, which is the temporary change in the way a circuit behaves due to an external excitation that will disappear with time.

S

step-down /stɛp daʊn/

ELECTRICAL POWER: TRANSFORMERS

ADJECTIVE A **step-down** transformer reduces a high voltage applied to the primary winding to a lower voltage on the secondary winding.

○ A step-down transformer is designed to reduce voltage from primary to secondary.

○ In a step-down transformer, the input voltage is greater than the output voltage.

step-up /stɛp ʌp/

ELECTRICAL POWER: TRANSFORMERS

ADJECTIVE A **step-up** transformer increases a low voltage applied to the primary winding to a higher voltage on the secondary winding.

○ Step-up transformers are used at electric power generating plants to develop very high voltages.

○ Step-up transformers are large expensive inductive transformers capable of converting low generator voltage into the operating voltage of the utility grid to inject energy into the grid system.

sub|sta|tion /sʌbsteɪʃ°n/ (substations)

ELECTRICAL POWER: DISTRIBUTION

NOUN A **substation** is an installation at which electricity is received from one or more power stations for conversion from AC to DC, reducing the voltage, or switching before distribution by a low-tension network.

○ In an electric power distribution system, voltage regulators may be installed at a substation so that all customers receive steady voltage independent of how much power is drawn from the line.

○ At the substation, the voltage is stepped down to distribution levels and the power is fed into the distribution grid where it is sent to the final consumers.

sup|ply /səplaɪ/ (supplies)

ELECTRICAL POWER: GENERATION

NOUN An electrical **supply** is a source of electrical energy.

○ When a direct current supply is connected to the conductor, it is seen to move.

○ *In the event of a fault isolate the mains supply before attempting to open the unit.*

---

surge /sɜːrdʒ/ (surges)

ELECTRICAL POWER: POWER CONSUMPTION

NOUN A **surge** is a momentary wave of current or power in an electric circuit.

○ *Without the safeguard of a fuse or breaker, electrical surges could cause overheating or even fire.*

○ *If the fuse is too large, it may not blow when a surge occurs.*

---

sus|cep|tance /səsɛptəns/

GENERAL

NOUN **Susceptance** is a measure of how easy it is for alternating current to pass through a capacitance or an inductance.

○ *While reactance is the measure of how much a circuit reacts against change in current over time, susceptance is the measure of how much a circuit is susceptible to conducting a changing current.*

○ *The susceptance of a particular capacitor or inductor depends on the frequency.*

---

switch¹ /swɪtʃ/ (switches)

CIRCUITS / ELECTRICAL POWER / COMPUTING AND CONTROL

NOUN A **switch** is a mechanical, electrical, electronic, or optical device for opening or closing a circuit or for diverting energy from one part of a circuit to another.

○ *In most cases, all the switches in the breaker box will be set to the on position.*

○ *A switch is provided for selecting one or the other of the gain control signals to be fed back to the luminance signal amplifier to control the gain.*

---

switch² /swɪtʃ/ (switches, switched, switching)

CIRCUITS / ELECTRICAL POWER / COMPUTING AND CONTROL

VERB If you **switch** an electric current **on** or **off**, you cause it to start or stop flowing or to change its path by operating a switch.

○ *The static bypass switch can be used to switch from one source to another without interruption in the supply of power.*

○ *When the current in a circuit is switched off, the induced magnetic field begins to collapse.*

---

switch|board /swɪtʃbɔːrd/ (**switchboards**)

ELECTRICAL POWER: POWER CONSUMPTION

NOUN A **switchboard** is an assembly of switchgear for the control of power supplies in an installation or building.

○ *At the main switchboard the ground wire is connected to the neutral wire and also connected to a convenient grounding point such as a water pipe.*

○ *A circuit feeder is a circuit connected directly from the main low voltage switchboard to the major current-using equipment.*

---

switch|gear /swɪtʃɡɪər/

ELECTRICAL POWER: DISTRIBUTION

NOUN **Switchgear** is any of several devices used for opening and closing electric circuits, especially those that pass high currents.

○ *If the demand for power from the facility is greater than the power provided by the solar system, the switchgear will draw the additional power required from the utility feeds.*

○ *Circuit breakers are made in varying sizes, from small devices that protect an individual household appliance up to large switchgear designed to protect high voltage circuits feeding an entire city.*

---

switch|ing sta|tion /swɪtʃɪŋ steɪʃ°n/ (**switching stations**)

ELECTRICAL POWER: DISTRIBUTION

NOUN A **switching station** is equipment used to tie together two or more electric circuits through switches.

○ *In a switching station, the switches are selectively arranged to permit a circuit to be disconnected, or to change the electric connection between the circuits.*

○ *The switching surge caused by switching off the extra high-voltage switching station will transmit rapidly along the direction of the large generators and the end of the transmission lines.*

syn|chro /sɪŋkroʊ/ (**synchros**)

COMPUTING AND CONTROL

NOUN A **synchro** is any of a number of electrical devices in which the angular position of a rotating part is transformed into a voltage, or vice versa.

○ The rotating antenna was repeated by a synchro receiver that rotated the magnetic deflection yoke about the neck of the CRT display, keeping the display synchronized with the direction of the antenna.

○ A synchro is a type of rotary electrical transformer sensor that is used for measuring the angle of a rotating machine such as an antenna platform.

syn|chro|nous con|vert|er /sɪŋkrənəs kənvɜrtər/ (**synchronous converters**)

ELECTRICAL POWER: MOTOR OR GENERATOR

NOUN A **synchronous converter** is a synchronous machine that converts alternating current to direct current, or vice versa.

○ A synchronous converter in which motor and generator windings are combined on one armature and excited by one magnetic field is normally used to change alternating to direct current.

○ For low power devices, synchronous converters have been replaced by solid state device equivalents.

syn|chro|nous ma|chine /sɪŋkrənəs məʃin/ (**synchronous machines**)

ELECTRICAL POWER: MOTOR OR GENERATOR

NOUN A **synchronous machine** is an electrical machine whose rotating speed is proportional to the frequency of the alternating current supply and independent of the load.

○ A rotary electric machine whose rotor rotates in synchronization with a rotating field that has been produced by an AC current flowing through a stator winding, is called a synchronous machine.

○ Since the induction motor has no DC field winding, there is no sustained field current in the rotor to provide flux as is the case with a synchronous machine.

syn|chro|nous speed /sɪŋkrənəs spiːd/

ELECTRICAL POWER: MOTOR OR GENERATOR

NOUN **Synchronous speed** is mechanical speed related to the electrical frequency by a number of pairs of poles.

○ *Singly fed electric machines have an effective constant torque speed range up to synchronous speed for a given excitation frequency.*

○ *At no load, losses in the motor cause the rotor speed to be slightly less than the synchronous speed of the stator field.*

sys|tem on a chip /sɪstəm ɒn ə tʃɪp/ (**systems on a chip**)

SEMICONDUCTOR AND ELECTRONIC CIRCUITRY

NOUN A **system on a chip** combines most of a system's elements on a single integrated circuit or chip.

○ *This new USB-based system on a chip provides the bandwidth necessary to stream HD video reliably throughout an entire home, share media content, and utilize Web-based applications.*

○ *Recently large-scale mixed signal system on a chip design techniques have been rapidly developed to integrate a lot of analog and digital circuits and functions on the same chip.*

S

Tt

tel|e|vi|sion (ABBR **TV**) /tɛlɪvɪʒ³n/

COMMUNICATION

NOUN **Television** is the system for sending pictures and sound by electrical signals over a distance, so that people can receive them in their home.

○ In television transmission, three signals must be sent on the carrier: the audio, picture intensity, and picture chrominance.

○ Television signals are strongest when the station transmitting tower and the home receiving antenna are in line-of-sight.

tem|per|a|ture /tɛmprətʃər/

GENERAL

NOUN **Temperature** is the average kinetic energy of the atoms or molecules of a substance, perceived as how hot or cold it is, and measured in degrees Fahrenheit, Celsius, or Kelvin.

○ Some light fixtures require cooling fans to keep the temperature in safe range and good ventilation.

○ The extended operating temperature range of -40 degrees Celsius to +125 degrees Celsius ensures these amplifiers can be used in extreme conditions, such as those found in industrial applications.

TALKING ABOUT TEMPERATURE

If the temperature of something stays the same, it is **constant**, and if it changes a lot, it is **variable**.

If the temperature of something goes up, it **rises**, and if it goes down, it **drops** or **falls**.

---

t

ther|mo|cou|ple /θɜːrmoʊkʌpᵊl/ (thermocouples)

INSTRUMENTATION, MEASURING, AND TESTING: DEVICES

NOUN A **thermocouple** is a temperature sensor formed by the junction of two different metals, producing a voltage proportional to the difference in temperature between the hot junction and the cold junction.

○ *A resistor may act as a thermocouple, producing a small DC voltage differential across it due to the thermoelectric effect if its ends are at somewhat different temperatures.*

○ *There are several types of thermocouples, constructed from different metals and with differing temperature ranges and accuracies.*

ther|mo|stat /θɜːrməstæt/ (thermostats)

INSTRUMENTATION, MEASURING, AND TESTING: DEVICES

NOUN A **thermostat** is a type of circuit that shows whether a measured temperature is above or below a particular point, and is used for thermal protection and simple temperature control systems.

○ *When the thermostat isn't calling for the unit to be running, the coil releases and the contacts open causing the compressor and fan motor to stop.*

○ *Electronic thermostats are temperature regulating devices, integrating a solid state thermistor to an electronic comparator circuit for accurate temperature control.*

three-phase /θriː feɪz/

ELECTRICAL POWER

ADJECTIVE A **three-phase** electrical system, circuit, or device has, generates, or uses three alternating voltages of the same frequency.

○ *When transformers are designed for three-phase applications, with typically high power and high voltage, the designer has a choice about how the windings are configured.*

○ *Unbalanced three-phase circuits are indicated by abnormally high currents in one or more of the phases.*

tid|al pow|er /taɪdᵊl paʊər/

ELECTRICAL POWER: GENERATION

NOUN **Tidal power** is the use of the rise and fall of the tides of oceans to generate electric power.

○ *Tidal power is a form of hydropower that exploits the movement of water caused by tidal currents or the rise and fall in sea levels due to the tides.*

○ *In flood tidal power generation below the water level there are openings in the tidal barrage that have turbines in them.*

---

to|roid /tɔːrɔɪd/ (**toroids**)

CIRCUITS / ELECTRICAL POWER / COMPUTING AND CONTROL

NOUN A **toroid** is a circular core used in transformers, that is shaped like a donut.

○ *Toroids are better than cylindrical cores because the magnetic field is mostly confined to the core rather than spilling off the ends of a cylinder.*

○ *Longitudinal magnetic fields were produced by passing the requisite electric current through a set of copper windings applied to the toroid.*

> **OTHER TRANSFORMER PARTS INCLUDE:**
>
> lamination, winding, primary winding, secondary winding

---

trans|ceiv|er /trænsivər/ (**transceivers**)

COMMUNICATION

NOUN A **transceiver** is a device that contains both a transmitter and receiver.

○ *Almost every piece of modern amateur radio equipment is now a transceiver but there is an active market for pure radio receivers, mainly for shortwave listening operators.*

○ *Many authorities suggest not even turning on a transceiver without a 50-ohm load connected to its unused output.*

---

trans|duc|er /trænzdusər/ (**transducers**)

COMPUTING AND CONTROL

NOUN A **transducer** is an electronic device that converts energy from one form to another, just as a microphone converts sound to electrical energy.

○ *The input device, with a transducer in it, senses the quantity under measurement and changes it to a proportional electrical signal.*

○ *A transducer is a device that converts physical energy into an electrical voltage or current signal for transmission.*

> **WORD BUILDER**
> **trans-** = indicating change or movement
>
> The prefix **trans-** appears in several words meaning "changing" or "moving:" **transformer**, **transmission**, **transmit**, **transmitter**.

---

trans|fer /trænsfɜr/

COMPUTING AND CONTROL

NOUN **Transfer** is the amount of data that is transferred across a digital interface, not including any extra bits used to encode the data.

○ The standard addresses the need for very fast transfers of large volumes of information.

○ Low noise transfer of digital data is particularly beneficial in electrically noisy environments and for transmission over long distance.

---

trans|fer func|tion /trænsfɜr fʌŋkʃ³n/ (**transfer functions**)

COMPUTING AND CONTROL

NOUN The **transfer function** of a circuit is the ratio of the response to the input.

○ From a transfer function, you can directly get a Bode-Diagram or the steady state for a constant input.

○ Transfer functions are a well established convention for articulating a system response.

---

trans|form|er /trænsfɔrmər/ (**transformers**)

CIRCUITS / ELECTRICAL POWER / COMPUTING AND CONTROL

NOUN A **transformer** is an electrical device for changing the voltage of alternating current. The symbol for a transformer is xfmr.

○ By using transformers, the voltage of the power can be stepped up to a high voltage.

○ High resistance to electricity is desirable in the cores of transformers to reduce eddy currents.

> **TYPES OF TRANSFORMER INCLUDE:**
>
> autotransformer, current transformer, induction coil, isolation transformer

tran|si|ent /trænʃənt/

CIRCUITS / COMMUNICATION / COMPUTING AND CONTROL

ADJECTIVE If something is **transient**, it only lasts a short time, such as an electrical surge due to lightning.

○ *The transient voltage from a lightning strike may damage sensitive electronic equipment.*

○ *Light bulbs often fail on switch-on due to the sudden transient current induced in a cold lamp filament.*

▶ **COLLOCATIONS:**
  transient current
  transient load
  transient pulse

tran|si|ent re|sponse /trænʃənt rɪspɒns/ (**transient responses**)

CIRCUITS / COMMUNICATION / COMPUTING AND CONTROL

NOUN A **transient response** of a circuit is a temporary change in the way that it behaves due to an external excitation, that will disappear with time.

○ *Damping oscillation is a typical transient response where the output value oscillates until finally reaching a steady-state value.*

○ *The transient response shows the behavior of the regulator to a voltage change.*

tran|sis|tor /trænzɪstər/ (**transistors**)

ELECTRONICS COMPONENTS

NOUN A **transistor** is a basic solid-state control device that controls current flow between two terminals, based on the voltage or current delivered to a third terminal.

○ *The output transistor dumps any current which is not needed by the speaker, so when it is completely turned off, all the current source output flows through the speaker.*

○ *Power transistors drive the armature windings at a specified motor current and voltage level.*

trans|mis|sion /trænzmɪʃᵊn/

ELECTRICAL POWER: DISTRIBUTION

NOUN **Transmission** is the movement of large quantities of electric energy.

○ The first long-distance transmission of alternating current took place in 1891 in Colorado.

○ The required amount of rural transmission can be mitigated through the use of daily energy storage located close to the generators and the loads.

trans|mis|sion line /trænzmɪʃᵊn laɪn/ (**transmission lines**)

CIRCUITS / ELECTRICAL POWER

NOUN A **transmission line** is a system of conductors that transfers electrical signals from one place to another.

○ The rising and falling of the waves moves the buoy-like structure creating mechanical energy which is converted into electricity and transmitted to shore over a submerged transmission line.

○ The rural wind farm feeds an urban load via a long transmission line.

trans|mit /trænzmɪt/ (**transmits, transmitted, transmitting**)

COMMUNICATION

VERB If a device **transmits** power or a signal, it sends information, normally in the form of electrical signals. The symbol for transmit is Tx.

○ The high side is connected in a star configuration so that the power generated by the power plant can be transmitted over long distances economically.

○ The modem modulates a signal being transmitted and demodulates a signal being received.

▶ **COLLOCATIONS:**
transmit power
transmit a signal

trans|mit|ter /trænzmɪtər/ (**transmitters**)

COMMUNICATION

NOUN A **transmitter** is a circuit that accepts signals or data in and translates them into a form that can be transmitted, usually over a distance. The symbol for transmitter is either Tx or xmitter.

○ *A smaller variable inductor between the transmitter and the antenna feedthrough is used for fine tuning.*

○ *The dummy load is a safety backup to protect the transmitter if the control box should lose power while transmitting.*

RELATED WORDS

Compare **transmitter** with **receiver**, which is a circuit that accepts signals from a transmission medium and decodes or translates them into a form that can drive local circuits.

---

tur|bine /tɜrbaɪn/ (turbines)

ELECTRICAL POWER: GENERATION

NOUN A **turbine** is a machine that uses a moving stream of air, water, steam, or hot gas to turn a wheel to produce mechanical power.

○ *Should the wind turbine produce more power than the demand of the house, this excess power is fed into the grid via a meter which counts the units fed in.*

○ *Water is used as a coolant and moderator and turned directly into steam to drive the turbine which turns the generator.*

---

tur|bo-e|lec|tric /tɜrboʊ ɪlɛktrɪk/

ELECTRICAL POWER: GENERATION

ADJECTIVE A **turbo-electric** device or system is made by, related to, or uses an electric generator driven by a turbine.

○ *The advantage of turbo-electric transmissions is that they allow the adaptation of high-speed turning turbines to the slow turning propellers or wheels without the need of a heavy and complex gearbox.*

○ *Large steam powered turbo generators provide the majority of the world's electricity, and are also used by steam powered turbo-electric ships.*

▶ COLLOCATIONS:
turboelectric drive
turboelectric generator

tur|bo|gen|er|a|tor /tɜrboʊdʒɛnəreɪtər/ (**turbogenerators**)

NOUN A **turbogenerator** is a large electrical generator that is driven by a steam turbine.

  ○ *In case of a circuit failure with simultaneous loss of external power, power is supplied by the spinning down turbogenerators for about 45 seconds, during which time the diesel generators start up.*

  ○ *This turbogenerator combines a gas turbine engine with an electric generator on one shaft.*

twist|ed pair /twɪstɪd pɛər/ (**twisted pairs**)

NOUN A **twisted pair** is a pair of wires that are twisted together to reduce interference.

  ○ *The effect of stray magnetic fields can be minimized by using twisted pair leads and by avoiding loops in which an emf could be induced.*

  ○ *It is common for untwisted cables to couple RF into equipment when used as loudspeaker cable, and for the interference problems to be solved when it is replaced by an unshielded twisted pair.*

T

Uu

un|in|ter|rupt|i|ble pow|er sup|ply (ABBR UPS)
/ˌʌnɪntərˈʌptɪbᵊl ˈpaʊər səˈplaɪ/ (**uninterruptible power supplies**)

GENERAL

NOUN An **uninterruptible power supply** is a system where there is a back-up supply.

- An uninterruptible power supply is also permitted to supply emergency loads.

- An uninterruptible power supply is an electrical apparatus that provides emergency power to a load when the input power source, typically mains power, fails.

u

Vv

var|i|a|ble /vɛəriəbᵊl/

ADJECTIVE A **variable** electrical component or device is designed so that a particular property, such as resistance, can be varied.

○ Variable belt drives require precise alignment and careful setup to work efficiently.

○ A variable resistor is a resistor whose values can be changed or varied over a range.

ver|y high fre|quen|cy (ABBR VHF) /vɛri haɪ friːkwənsi/

NOUN **Very high frequency** is used to describe radio frequencies in the range 30 MHz to 300 MHz.

○ FM radio signals are carried by very high frequency radio waves (88 to 108 MHz).

○ The switching control circuit causes the switching devices to switch On and Off in an alternating manner at a very high frequency.

volt (ABBR V) /voʊlt/ (volts)

NOUN A **volt** is a unit of measurement for electromotive force, expressing the electric tension or the difference in charge between two points. The symbol for voltage is either V or E.

○ Volts measure the electrical potential between two points.

○ On the terminals of the condenser the electromotive force was about 120 volts.

volt|age reg|u|la|tor /ˈvoʊltɪdʒ rɛɡyəleɪtər/ (**voltage regulators**)

CIRCUITS / ELECTRICAL POWER

NOUN A **voltage regulator** is a circuit that is connected between the power source and a load, that provides a constant voltage despite variations in input voltage or output load.

○ *When used with a voltage regulator, the compensator can automatically run overexcited at times of high load and underexcited at light loads.*

○ *The low voltage measurement is not really necessary, but is useful when the battery is low, so you can be sure the voltage regulator is still doing its job.*

▶ **SYNONYM:**
load regulator

volt|am|me|ter /ˈvoʊltæmmɪtər/ (**voltammeters**)

INSTRUMENTATION, MEASURING, AND TESTING: INSTRUMENT

NOUN A **voltammeter** is an instrument that can measure both volts and amps.

○ *The DC resistance of each phase of each winding is measured separately by the voltammeter.*

○ *A voltammeter measures both electrical current and voltage by weighing the element deposited or released at the cathode during a particular period of time.*

> **WORD BUILDER**
> **-meter** = measuring instrument
>
> The suffix **-meter** is often used for instruments that measure things: **accelerometer**, **ammeter**, **multimeter**, **voltmeter**.

volt-am|pere /ˈvoʊltæmpɪər/ (**volt-amperes**)

CIRCUITS / ELECTRICAL POWER

NOUN A **volt-ampere** is the voltage times the current feeding an electrical load.

○ *A volt-ampere is the unit used for the apparent power in an electrical circuit, equal to the product of voltage and current.*

v

○ The overcurrent protection is not to exceed 167 percent of the power source current rating determined by dividing the power-source volt-ampere rating by the rated output voltage.

---

volt|me|ter /vˈoʊltmitər/ (**voltmeters**)

INSTRUMENTATION, MEASURING, AND TESTING: INSTRUMENT

NOUN A **voltmeter** is an instrument that can measure volts.

○ Check the voltage used on the bulb with a voltmeter.

○ For storing energy from a solar cell, you need to check the voltage output by the solar cell under sunlight using a voltmeter.

V|S|W|R /viˈ ɛs dˈʌbᵊlyu ˈɑr/ (short for **voltage standing wave ratio**, **vertical standing wave ratio**)

SEMICONDUCTOR AND ELECTRONIC CIRCUITRY

ABBREVIATION **VSWR** is a measure of how efficiently radio-frequency power is transmitted from a power source, through a transmission line, and into a load.

○ In a properly set-up transmission system the VSWR is near to one.

○ The VSWR can be measured using a slotted line in which a probe can be placed to determine the maximum and minimum voltages.

V

Ww

---

watt (ABBR **W**) /wɒt/ (**watts**)

GENERAL

NOUN A **watt** is a unit of power, equal to a power rate of one joule of work per second of time.

- A 100 watt amplifier would have to be reduced to 10 in order for an audio perception of a sound level to be cut in half.
- The average person in the US consumes 60 barrels of oil per year and on average this is 10,000 watts of power consumption.

> **WORD ORIGINS**
>
> This word is named for **James Watt** (1736–1819), the Scottish engineer.

---

wave farm /weɪv fɑrm/ (**wave farms**)

ELECTRICAL POWER: GENERATION

NOUN A **wave farm** is a collection of machines designed to generate electricity by using the energy of ocean waves.

- Wave power generation is still in an experimental stage of development and the world's first commercial wave farm began in 2008 in Portugal.
- The wave farm has three wave energy converters which are producing a total of 2.25MW.

---

wave|form /weɪvfɔrm/ (**waveforms**)

CIRCUITS / COMMUNICATION / COMPUTING AND CONTROL

NOUN A **waveform** is the graphic representation of how a quantity such as voltage varies under particular circumstances or over time.

○ *The oscilloscope is helpful in determining if the amplitude of the input waveform needs to be increased.*

○ *There are two types of waveform available from high-quality inverters – the modified sine wave and the true sine wave.*

---

wave pow|er /weɪv paʊər/

ELECTRICAL POWER: GENERATION

NOUN **Wave power** is power created by the movement of ocean waves.

○ *In general, larger waves are more powerful but wave power is also determined by wave speed, wavelength, and water density.*

○ *When the significant wave height is given in meters, and the wave period in seconds, the result is the wave power in kilowatts per meter of wavefront length.*

---

we|ber (ABBR **Wb**) /wɛbər/ (**webers**)

GENERAL

NOUN A **weber** is a unit that is used to measure magnetic flux.

○ *Flux is a product of the average component of magnetic induction perpendicular to any given surface in a magnetic field by the area of that surface, expressed in webers.*

○ *A uniform change of one weber per second in flux linking a one-turn winding will generate one volt across it.*

> **WORD ORIGINS**
>
> This word is named for **Wilhelm Eduard Weber** (1804–1891), the German physicist who, along with Carl Friedrich Gauss, invented the first electromagnetic telegraph.

Wi|Fi /waɪ faɪ/

COMMUNICATION: DIGITAL

ABBREVIATION **Wi-Fi** is a form of wireless connection that is used with computers and phones.

○ *You can work almost anywhere by using a mobile Wi-Fi device to connect to the Internet.*

○ *Dual stream capability allows consumers the flexibility to place their Wi-Fi enabled HD video system wherever it suits their needs and still enjoy an uninterrupted high-quality viewing experience.*

wind farm /wɪnd fɑrm/ (**wind farms**)

ELECTRICAL POWER: GENERATION

NOUN A **wind farm** is a large group of wind-driven generators for electricity supply.

○ *The company will optimize a wind farm layout for energy yield given turbine spacing, setback distances, shadow flicker, and acoustic noise level constraints.*

○ *For a wind farm, the capacity factor is mostly determined by the availability of wind.*

wind|ing /waɪndɪŋ/ (**windings**)

CIRCUITS / ELECTRICAL POWER

NOUN A **winding** is one or more turns of wire that forms a continuous coil through which an electric current can pass, as used in transformers and generators.

○ *These chargers use an autotransformer in which the primary and secondary windings are electrically connected.*

○ *There are two windings in a current transformer, one of them is a high current primary and the other is a low current secondary.*

wind pow|er /wɪnd pauər/

ELECTRICAL POWER: GENERATION

NOUN **Wind power** is power produced from windmills and wind turbines.

○ *To achieve maximum wind power, the owners decided to construct the turbines along a place on the ridge that reaches an elevation of about 1,200 ft.*

○ *In addition to large wind farms connected to transmission networks, smaller wind farms and individual wind power plants connected to distribution networks, are being built.*

W

wire¹ /waɪər/ (**wires**)

CIRCUITS / ELECTRICAL POWER / COMPUTING AND CONTROL

NOUN A **wire** is a flexible metallic conductor, especially one made of copper, usually insulated, and used to carry electric current in a circuit.

○ Most outdoor fuseboxes have a protective cover on the outside and inside to prevent rain from touching the wires.

○ In the event of a fault, the ground wire can carry enough current to blow a fuse and isolate the faulty circuit.

wire² /waɪər/ (**wires, wired, wiring**)

GENERAL

VERB If you **wire** an electrical system, circuit, or component, you equip it with wires.

○ The test should be repeated at every outlet to ensure that the downstream outlets are also wired correctly.

○ Several lamps were wired in series for use on standard voltage circuits.

wir|ing /waɪərɪŋ/

GENERAL

NOUN **Wiring** is the network of wires used in an electrical system, device, or circuit.

○ Electricians should preserve the polarity of the wiring when they install outlets in new homes.

○ The circuit breaker works as a protection whenever electrical wiring in a building has too much current flowing through it.

W

Zz

ZIF /zɪf/ (short for **zero insertion force**)

| SEMICONDUCTOR AND ELECTRONIC CIRCUITRY |

ABBREVIATION **ZIF** describes a type of microchip socket that clamps the chip pins after insertion, and so requires no downward force on the microchip or its pins to insert it into the socket.

○ ZIF is especially useful in applications in which repeated insertions subject the IC or the socket to wear and breakage.

○ ZIF is a chip socket that allows you to insert and remove a chip without special tools.

9 780007 489794